MAKE WAVES!

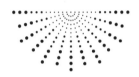

HAL ROBERTS

Published by EduMatch®
PO Box 150324, Alexandria, VA 22315
www.edumatch.org

These books are available at special discounts when purchased in quantities of 10 or more for use as premiums, promotions fundraising, and educational use. For inquiries and details, contact the publisher: sarah@edumatch.org.

ISBN: 9781970133332

CONTENTS

Acknowledgments   v

Introduction   vii

1. We Are Chosen to Produce Fruit   1
2. What is your Passion?   11
3. "Assessment" Is Not a Bad Word   25
4. You Must Have Perseverance!   37
5. Drench Yourself In Every Aspect of Your Job   51
6. Build Safe & Healthy Relationships   61
7. There is No Such Thing As A Minor Lapse of   75
   Integrity
8. Authority: The Buck Stops on Your Desk   85
9. Change Is Hard   103
10. Trust Is Never Owned — It's Only Rented   113
11. There Is Magic In Enthusiasm & Excitement   123
12. Humility Is Showing Vulnerability   135
13. Empowering Others is Real Leadership   145
14. Lead to Serve   157
15. We Must be Kindlers of Hope   165
16. Aim for Significance Over Greatness   175
    Afterword   187
    Conclusion   189

APPENDIX
The "Umami" Lesson Plan   199
The Perfect Lesson Plan Template   207
Move your Students from Consumption to   211
Creation
Training & Professional Development   215

References   219

Other EduMatch Titles   225

ACKNOWLEDGMENTS

I have so many to thank, as this book is truly a collaboration of some of the best and brightest educational leaders in the country from my professional learning network on Twitter.

I am so grateful for my helpmate of almost forty-four years, my beautiful wife, Susan. She inspires me every day to be a better man, husband, father, grandfather, and Christian. I also thank her for her countless hours of editing this entire book as I could not have written it without her assistance and encouragement.

INTRODUCTION

I began my last introduction with,

"I have never attempted anything more fearful in my life than writing this book. I have punted out of the end zone against the Dallas Cowboys in Texas Stadium, punted against the Green Bay Packers, played in Bryant–Denny Stadium in Alabama, and competed in the first University of Houston vs. Rice football game in a sold-out Rice stadium (72,000+) in my first collegiate game. All of those experiences would be quite fearful to many people. However, I loved competing at the professional and collegiate level, and I just wished my professional career would have lasted more than one year. I would not trade that experience for the world."

This one may be more fearful, since this time I have written what I believe is a much better book. Have you ever handed something in/made a speech/given a presentation and thought, "I wish I would have...?" This is where I began this work. So now, I begin.

Bill Clinton and George W. Bush agree on this: "Learning leadership skills is crucial in just about every worthwhile endeavor in American life, political and otherwise."

Writing a book, as a friend told me, is like baring your soul. That is precisely what this book is, my soul as a leader, my 38 years of experience, and a collaboration with some of the best educational leaders in this country. As I initially took on this challenge, I e-mailed many of my Twitter personal learning network (PLN) colleagues to help me. Since I did this, I have researched and read over twenty books on leadership, change-makers, and neuroscience.

This book is my conviction of what it takes to be the best leader you can become. This credo will work with leading a family, company, class, school, athletic team, church, or any group of people. "Making waves" sometimes has a negative connotation, but if you Google *make waves,* the first definition that is listed is "create a significant impression." That is my mission of this book—to make you a leader that creates a *significant* impression.

I wanted to set sail in more uncharted waters. As I thought, I consulted with a couple of my PLN of #CelebratEd friends who helped me come up with this title, *Make Waves!* I owe a huge debt of gratitude to Melissa Rathmann (@MelissaRathmann) and Jeff Kubiak (@jeffreykubiak) in helping me.

So here I am, writing about the attributes of a Wave-Making leader. In the fall of 2014, one of my former student/athletes, Edward Crouch (pastor of Summit Heights Fellowship), invited me to speak at his church. It was then, as I prepared and researched my sermon, that I came up with several chapter titles in this book. As a result, I will reference the apostle Paul and his voyage to Rome, and I call him the first *Wave-Maker*. He definitely did not follow tradition and eventually gave his life for what he believed. In addition, he had many leadership qualities that I will convey in most of the chapters. Reflecting on my study and research, I have included sixteen attributes that I think illustrate a comprehensive picture of what a *Wave-Making* leader should possess. I asked my pastor, Josh Howerton of LakePointe Church, what he saw Paul's leadership attributes were. This was his reply:

"Paul's attributes that made him a spiritual leader... He was

PRIMARILY a follower and SECONDARILY a leader. He followed Christ before he led people. That's what separates a spiritual leader from a leader. Paul had a bias toward action— he was decisive and tended toward DOING rather than paralysis by analysis and overthinking. He was strategic. Paul targeted large cities in Rome, knowing if he could penetrate cities with the gospel, the message would flow throughout the empire. He was a developer of people. He ALWAYS had someone with him he was bringing along, pouring into, and he was writing to leaders he was developing. "

This is my story, and I tried to draw upon my faith, my experiences, and my relationships. There are many biblical examples and scripture references that confirm what I am trying to convey. However, no matter what your beliefs are, the attributes or lessons that I speak about can be applied to anyone who leads a family, church, company, classroom, campus, team, or organization.

This book is similar to the rudder on your vessel, the GPS in your car, and the compass in your hands. The compass relies on one true north, and that true north never changes. Maybe these words can be your guide, similar to your true north. You are the one that has the steering wheel, the helm in your hands. You are the one who steers or decides the direction.

I do not know what your mission is or what goals you have set, but the following chapters are not written lightly or just on theory. They have been proven by me in practice, and virtually all have been verified by research. As you read, please think of your organization and how you can infuse each of the sixteen attributes of leadership. I wish I could have had *Make Waves!* when I began my leadership journey.

So there you have it; my research and collaboration of over almost five years with the help of the best and brightest educators in the country. Leadership is difficult, but it is also enriching. So join me as we sail away from safe harbors into the rough, sometimes treacherous, challenging, but never dull waters of leadership. I pray that your voyage can be as rewarding and blessed as mine has been.

I also pray that my words can assist, inspire, and edify you as you "set sail" on your own journey of leadership, and dream His dreams, explore His will and discover His purpose for you. Allow His story to change your story! Make Waves!

Don't be traditional—rock the boat & make waves!

Your school/team/organization/class rises & falls on your leadership!

Make waves — *create a significant impression; to do something innovative that draws a large amount of attention and makes a widespread impact on its society, industry, etc.; sometimes a little controversial.*

WE ARE CHOSEN TO PRODUCE FRUIT

It isn't the farm that makes the farmer, it's the love, hard work, and character. —Unknown

The connoisseur does not drink wine but tastes its secrets.— Salvador Dali

Wine cheers the sad, revives the old, inspires the young, makes weariness forget his toil.—Lord Byron

Farming is a profession of hope.—Unknown

#LifeisaCabernet!—Hashtag for Silver Oak wine

Wine is sunlight, held together by water.—Galileo Galilei

You can't buy happiness, but you can buy wine, and that's kind of the same thing.—Unknown

We are all farmers, winegrowers, and vintners. We prepare the soil by tilling it and make it as fertile as we can. We plant seeds. We fertilize and water those seeds. Sometimes we must count on God to give us good weather: sun but not too much, rain enough for our crops and vines to grow. Then we wait... we wait to see how each of our investments multiplies as we see our kids graduate. If we are lucky, we have students come back to thank us and tell how we impacted their lives. It is then that we realize why we do what we do!

A few summers ago, my wife and I visited the wine country in Napa, California. This trip was on my bucket list, and I learned more than I could have imagined. We visited several vineyards, seeing a variety of grapes and sampling various types of wines. In the process, I learned about the tastes we all experience, which are sweet, sour, salty, bitter, and the one I had never heard before — umami. (See my Umami Lesson Plan in the Appendix for a detailed explanation.)

When farmers get together, sometimes they complain. They complain about the cost of equipment. They complain about the cost of fuel. They complain about the cost of fertilizer.

Sometimes they complain about the weather. They complain about droughts. They complain about too much rain. They complain about how insects impact their crops. However, they rarely complain about the cost of seeds, realizing that buying seeds is an investment. Most of what they complain about is out of their control. However, they know that the seeds they plant will multiply over and over again. You see, it is our investment in kids' lives where we must focus.

Speaking of supplies, teachers are unique in that we are the only profession where you steal supplies from home and bring them to work. Almost without exception, if a teacher needs supplies that are not provided by the school, they will go and purchase them with their own money. I do not think this happens in any other profession! We also know the seeds that we sow are our focus, rather than the debt that we owe.

We, educators, know that no seed = no harvest. We also know that if we plant hope, ambition and success will grow. If we plant grit, a person of commitment will grow. If we plant honesty, integrity will be harvested. So you see, what we plant daily is of utmost importance. It is the investment of enhancing kids' lives that we must commit to a daily mission. We must be intentional every day because every day matters.

Unity is the soul of culture. Destroy it, and you rip the heart out of the campus/district. It is the essence, the core of how a healthy organization should function. The holy trinity

(Father, Son, Holy Spirit) is the perfect example of sacrificial love, humble other-centeredness, and perfect harmony. The grapevine trinity is another example, the vine, branches, and grapes are all one, but different and with their own function —but each part needs each other.

Wine-making includes a plethora of terms (much like education), and one of my favorites is *terroir*. The term itself comes from the Latin word for land (*terra*), and it describes four factors—soil, climate, terrain, and culture—that shape the character of wine to give rise to a unique flavor that reflects its origins. Because vines and grapes are incredibly responsive to their environment, even small variations across any of the four factors can have a dramatic impact on how they taste. Try to stretch your imagination to this illustration as I equate wine-making to enhancing students' lives. One can see how culture, pedagogy, kindling hope, and relationships have a dramatic impact on a student's life, much like terroir does to wine.

Vines naturally spread or crawl along the ground. However, if this happens with grapes, they will not grow or bear fruit. If they stay there, they get dirty; rain makes them muddy and mildewed, and they become sick and useless. When that happens, the winegrower *lifts them up*, washes them off and attaches them to a trellis so that they can cling. Isn't our job to lift up others (our students)? With care and feeding, they will thrive. They climb and eventually cluster into abundant fruit.

Follow me in this analogy, as I compare teaching and leading to farming and viticulture. Sometimes the seeds are our words, objectives, and vision. The soil could be our culture in which our students are immersed. Soil could also be the rigorous curriculum that we teach our kids. The fertilizer can be the hope that we kindle each day. So you see, the farming and grape-growing analogy to education can be easily visualized and is all-encompassing.

As we walked among the vineyards, I wanted to know more about grapes and vines. The author of *The Wine Bible,* Karen MacNeil, is a brilliant wordsmith who writes about wine. As you read, think how similar education/teaching are.

I love wine because it is one of the last true things. In a world digitized to distraction, a world where you can't get out of our pajamas without your cell phone, wine remains utterly primary...wine matters because of this ineluctable connection. Wine and food cradle us in our own communal humanity. Anthropologically, they are the pleasures that carried life forward and sustained through the sometimes dark days of our own evolution. Drinking wine, then—as small as that action can seem —is both grounding and transformative. It reminds us of other things that matter, too: love, friendship, generosity.

I have a cork from Bogle Winery that on the side of it reads, "In water, one sees one's own face, but in wine, one beholds the heart of another."

I found that a vine does four things: it crawls, clings, climbs, and clusters. I believe that we can visualize our change-makers exercising those four activities, as well. They crawl before they can walk/run in learning our objectives. They cling to whatever gives them love. They climb with the one who gives them hope. They cluster with their community, their neighbor, their peers, and their classroom with whom they identify. Through my experience, a great wine evokes an emotional response. And it is through emotion that the gateway to the brain opens and enhances long-term memory. So you see, wine, vineyards, farming, and viticulture align quite nicely with education and teaching.

When I researched farming and wine-making, I found that it is all about the fruit of labor. You see, there is always fruit (or crop) that is produced unless there are outside influences that prevent it from growing. There are droughts, insects, or diseases that could thwart the final fruit from coming to fruition. I have tasted sweet grapes and sour grapes. We all desire a sweet fruitful, harvest.

I am reminded of how scripture addresses producing the sweetest fruit in John 15.

The setting takes place right after the Last Supper as Jesus led his disciples to a nearby vineyard. He had just finished washing the feet of his disciples, even the one who would betray him later, to demonstrate the importance of serving others. This message was His last before He was put to death on a cross. Just imagine Jesus, speaking to His disciples as He is in the midst of a vineyard and maybe crouching down and pointing and even handling a cluster of grapes.

I am the Real Vine, and my Father is the Farmer. He lifts up every branch apart of me that doesn't bear grapes. And every branch that is grape-bearing he prunes back so it will bear even more. You are already pruned back by the message I have spoken.

Live in me. Make your home in me just as I do in you. In the same way that a branch can't bear grapes by itself but only by being joined to the vine, you can't bear fruit unless you are joined with me.

I am the Vine, you are the branches. When you're joined with me, and I with you, the relation intimate and organic, the harvest is sure to be abundant. Separated, you can't produce a thing. Anyone who separates from me is gathered (lifted) up and at times thrown on the bonfire. But if you make yourselves at home with me and my words are at home in you, you can be sure that whatever you ask will be listened to and acted upon. This is how my Father shows who he is—when you produce grapes, when you mature as my disciples.

I've loved you the way my Father has loved me. Make yourselves at home in my love. If you keep my commands, you'll remain intimately at home in my love. That's what I've done—kept my Father's commands and made myself at home in his love.

I've told you these things for a purpose: that my joy might be your joy, and your joy wholly mature. This is my command: Love one another the way I loved you. This is the very best way to love. Put your life on the line for your friends. You are my friends when you do the things I command you. I'm no longer calling you servants because servants don't understand what their master is thinking and planning. No, I've named you friends because I've let you in on everything I've heard from the Father.

You didn't choose me, remember; I chose you, and put
you in the world to bear fruit, fruit that won't spoil. As
fruit bearers, whatever you ask the Father in relation to
me, he gives you.

But remember the root command: Love one another.

—John 15: 1-17 (MSG)

One thing we must remember, the vinedresser/farmer never
leaves his vines/crop alone. He is always in a constant *relationship* with his vine or crop. Sometimes he has to prune
away branches that are not producing or to take away the
branches or leaves that prevent sunlight to the more abundant
branches. And when he prunes, he is never closer to the vine.
Our job is all about producing fruit—abundant, sweet-tasting,
successful fruit. We do whatever it takes for a successful and
plentiful harvest.

Farming, grape-growing, and wine-making take constant care
in producing the best fruit or crop possible. Farmers work
year-round to ensure productivity and quality. Many wines
that I know use more than one grape (and often several) to
produce the best wine possible. The ultimate goal is to
produce grapes that mature gradually, yielding complex and
concentrated flavors. An art that winemakers also practice,
which often puts their special signature on a wine, is that of

blending: mixing various wines to achieve the desired style, complexity, and balance.

As educators, we must persistently tweak, assess, and determine what is best for each of our students. Teachers create their lessons that have depth and complexity. Each lends her artistic touch to each lesson she teaches. We know that one size does not fit all. We lay our best foundation, "lift up" each student, give them hope so that they can grow, and mature to reach their potential.

When we begin to load our boat for our leadership voyage, producing fruit may be our lightest load. It is so rewarding to witness our kids grow. However, we must be intentional every day and every period. Remember that we have 180 days to impact, love, and kindle hope for the change-makers we teach. Make every day intentional to make a difference in the trajectory of the rest of a child's life. Make Waves!

MAKING WAVES

Robert Mondavi (a famous winemaker in Napa, California) said, "Making a good wine is a skill; making a fine wine is an art." Isn't this what teaching and leading are all about? Combining our skills and our own way (our art) in enhancing kids' lives. Put *your* mark or brand on your position. Find a way to create a significant impression.

2

WHAT IS YOUR PASSION?

Develop a passion for learning. If you do, you will never cease to grow. —Anthony J. D'Angelo

A great leader's courage to fulfill his vision comes from passion, not position.—John Maxwell

Chase down your passion like it's the last bus of the night.

Passion is simply a heart issue.

Passion results from your purpose.

Leadership is hard! To get results, leadership matters. If you don't have a passion for leading your crew, you will experience misery and probably will not last, much less succeed and inspire.

My friend Angela Maiers's (@angelamaiers) statement on passion is one that I use in my presentations and expresses passion very well.

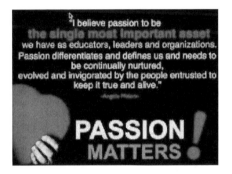

A good friend and colleague of mine, Daisy Dyer Duerr (@daisydyerduerr), former Principal of Saint Paul K-12 schools (2014 Bammy Awards nominee and NASSP Digital Principal Award Winner), says,

Educational leadership is my passion; it's not my job, it's not my profession, it's my passion. Leadership is challenging; think about the things you are passionate about in your life; family, love, hobbies (sports for me), are those easy? NO!

They are a constant challenge, at least for me they always have been, a very worthwhile challenge. As I "sail" on my journey through educational leadership, I say bring on the rough seas (challenges)! We live this life as passionate educators, putting our students above all else, making daring decision in the face of criticism because it's what's best for kids. I want to be a leader that my students, staff, teachers, and community know will listen to them, take chances for them, and be willing to fail and recover from it for the greater good!

She continues:

In leadership, we have a choice; stay the course and get the same results we have always gotten...or take risks and possibly get rewards. We need trailblazers, we need leaders that will take risks, even fail in search of "treasure"—the greater good of our changemakers and schools.

Black Bart and other *Wave Makers* always talked of
being powerful. To me, the key to that in leadership is
not in being powerful, but rather being empowering.
None of us can steer our ships alone, we need as many
strong mates by our sides as possible, which is why I
choose to Make Waves! Bring on the rough seas! The
rougher the seas, the smoother we sail! Ahoy!

I will add that leading is not our job, it's our passion. Getting
better at it—that's our job. After a long board meeting, one of
my board members shared, "I could see your passion come
through as you were talking." Hopefully, through the years,
most of my stakeholders were able to see my passion through
my words and actions every day.

One way you can determine if you are passionate about your
job is to consider if you look forward to everything that the
job entails. I'm not so naive to think that every day you will
have a great day, simply because you have passion for your
area of service. You will experience valleys, but with passion,
there will be many more summits. I'm sure many of you
think, "I wish my staff knew the hours that I put in my week
to keep this organization running smoothly." It is passion that
drives you to accomplish things you thought you could not do.
It is through passion that you will find your purpose in life. It
is passion that will not allow you to "settle" on anything.

Passion will give you that energy that is absolutely needed to work 60, 70, or 80 hours a week. It gives you that shot of adrenaline when it is most needed. Also, it will give you credibility. When you do what you love and love what you do, others find that inspiring. When you show your passion, you touch the emotions of your followers.

Neuroscience says that touching emotions is the gateway to the brain and long-term memory. When you tap into your passion, you can share experiences or stories that exhibit that passion. The brain loves a good story. A story is one of the best ways to touch emotions. So share your personal experiences with your crew. One of the best storytellers of all time was Jesus. The disciples asked why he told so many stories. He replied,

---

You've been given insight into God's kingdom. You know how it works. Not everybody has this gift, this insight; it hasn't been given to them. Whenever someone has a ready heart for this, the insights and understandings flow freely. But if there is no readiness, any trace of receptivity soon disappears. That's why I tell stories: to create readiness, to nudge the people toward receptive insight. In their present state they can stare till doomsday and not see it, listen till they're blue in the face and not get it.—Matt. 13:10–13, MSG

Stories engage your crew with what you are trying to convey, and then they start to buy into your vision. It is important to understand that your followers buy into you before they buy into your vision.

It is the job of the leader to show or exhibit this passion so that your crew can glean from it. Passion is contagious.

As I think about passionate people, my wife, Susan, comes to mind. She is a retired educator after 33 years spent in the classroom. Most of that time, she taught English and some speech, but was fortunate to have been asked to teach an AVID (Advancement Via Individual Determination) elective class her last couple of years. The change-makers in her class referred to her as their "AVID Momma." She was also the campus coordinator, as well as the district director. She did such a great job that she was asked to be a consultant—teaching teachers the AVID way. She continues to present to this day, after being retired for nine years. If you happen to follow her on Facebook, you will find that she continues to travel, conduct workshops, and present at AVID Summer Institutes. Her friends, colleagues, and family wonder why she continues to work. Her reply is simple: "I have a passion for what AVID represents and what it does for kids. I was able to see my students' lives changed as a result of AVID."

She then adds, "it changed my life too." As a result, she shares her passion, and every time she presents, participants either tell her or write in their evaluation that they can tell that she loves what she does and has a passion for it because it shows through her presentation.

As I visited classrooms, I always looked for the passion my teachers had, primarily for their students, and next for the content they were teaching. If they did not exhibit passion for what they were trying to teach, how did they expect their students would be interested or engaged in the lesson? I also looked for passion as I interviewed prospective teachers to my campus or district. I did not ask if they had passion—they had to show it to me. I could usually see it within the first ten minutes of the interview. Stephen Covey said, "If you can hire people whose passion intersects with the job, they won't require any supervision at all. They will manage themselves better than anyone could ever manage them. Their fire comes from within, not from without."

There will be days when some stakeholders call or visit and gripe about the decision(s) you made. There are times when your supervisor calls and tells you, "I need to see you." It is in these days that you may question your passion for leading. On these days you might ask yourself, "Would I be happier if I just went back into the classroom to teach?" This is when you have to dig down to search for some kind of passion to bring. This is when you have to ask yourself, "Why did I want to become a leader?" Let me tell you why I became a campus leader, which eventually led to leading an entire district.

I began my career as a seventh-grade health and social studies teacher and eighth-grade coach, just a couple of days before in-service started— I was working in a sporting goods store as a sales clerk when I met a person looking for a teacher/coach. I interviewed on a Friday and began working the following Monday. Since I played college football and spent a year in the National Football League, I (smugly) felt that I could coach junior high football! (There is a lot more to this story as I had a lot to learn in coaching.) Heck, I spent hours in NFL film rooms studying film, identifying secondary coverage, learning offensive plays, and calling blocking assignments as I read defensive fronts in punt formation. I felt completely confident and had no worries. Confidence, I had!

I still remember a veteran teacher pulling me to the side and giving me this sage advice: "Don't try to be friends with them, or they will walk all over you. I try not to smile for the first few weeks to make sure I get them under control." I just smiled, thanked her, and walked away. You see, I definitely had a passion for football and most other sports. So even in the classroom, I could always tell a football story to capture the emotions of my students. (I had no idea that this was actually using neuroscience—that as I captured their emotions, I got them engaged!) I know teachers who have a love of music, so they find some way to play music, play a musical instrument, or even sing as they present different topics (and they are not a choral/music teacher).

As I moved up the coaching ladder, I eventually reached my goal of becoming Head Football Coach and Athletic Director. I quickly found out that being the head coach was not all it was cracked up to be. I coached in a midsized district. My staff and I would coach our hearts out—and almost win. You see, as most of you know, as a head coach, you are measured by wins and losses. The superintendent who hired me jokingly said when I was first introduced, "we are with you, win or tie." Little did I know that was so true. I continued my career as an athletic director for ten years. I eventually went back to school to obtain my master's degree in secondary education. I told myself, "I don't think I will ever become a principal because I don't want to lose contact with my students."

I decided to pursue the principal position when I saw the school where my wife taught completely turn from a really good school to a really bad school in just one year as a result of one school leader. I realized that the leader has a huge impact on the direction, the culture, the standard, or success of the school or any business. A school campus, district, or any organization rises and falls on the leader.

What ignites your passion as a leader? Is it your love for

students? Finding different technology to enhance learning? Curriculum? Your love of_____? You can always share some kind of passion that you have. In the past couple of years, I have developed a passion for educational neuroscience—how the brain learns. I have immersed myself in many books on neuroscience and how it relates to leadership. I even moderated a Twitter chat with two international presenters and authors on neuroscience, Julie Adams and LaVonna Roth. (Now if I can just rise to their level of presenting, I will think I have made it!) I have even developed an entire presentation on this topic. You can view this presentation at https://youtu.be/obypkgdTaG8.

You do not have to know everything. You just need to know how to get the job done. For example, there are probably not many of you who are passionate about creating a master schedule. This is when can you do a great job of hiring or delegating people around you who are good at details and know the science of making a master schedule. Probably most of you are passionate about seeing your kids in extracurricular activities. As a former athlete, I loved seeing my kids compete in any activity. I obviously loved watching my students in sports. However, I developed a love for theater when my daughter participated in theater in high school. In Texas, there is a competition called the One-Act Play, where students perform a production lasting between 18 and 40 minutes. In one high school I led, our One Act Play won the state championship. I was as thrilled to experience that as I would have been watching a state football championship! It is the largest high school play production contest or play festival in the world (a perfect example of "everything is bigger in Texas"). My daughter found her passion there and went on to major in theater arts in college.

Late in my career (in fact, my last year as superintendent), I developed a passion for persuading my teachers to integrate technology in their pedagogy. I wanted my teachers to participate in "interactive faculty meetings," not just "sit and get." I only presented different technology applications to use in the classroom, for example, having a QR code hunt. It was rather simple, as I posted several QR codes around the cafeteria. I used the Remind app to tell my teachers to download a QR reader on their iPads. When they entered the cafeteria, they were met with an initial QR code which gave them directions. At this station, I provided an answer sheet to record their answers as they made their way around the room. This was a fun way to introduce QR codes to my teachers. I had "Appy Hour," where a couple of teachers would present their favorite apps and how they used them in their classroom. I thought it was far more effective for teachers to see their colleagues present this type of information. So you see, you can even develop a new passion after you become a leader. We are all lifelong learners, so the chances of finding another passion are completely possible and even probable.

Former PGA tour great Greg Norman, aka "the Shark," has many business ventures outside of golf. He is one of the most successful former professional athletes after his competitive playing career. One of his many businesses is golf apparel. I am a loyal customer of his shirts. As I was looking at his shirts one day, I noticed a tag with his shark logo and brand. It said, "#ATTACKLIFE...is an attitude and a call to action. It's about passion for performance and playing to win, on and off the course. I always attack life. They don't call me the shark for nothing." That attitude, we all could follow, not only in the way we lead our organizations but life in as well.

The apostle Paul is a perfect example of leadership. You will see examples of his leading throughout this book. I label him as the Original *Wave-Maker* and outline his *wave-making* attributes as a leader.

Paul's journey to Rome took him across the Mediterranean Sea, which (scholars believe) took several weeks to complete. Some say that this record in Acts 27 is one of the most informative accounts of ancient nautical travel than any other first-century source. Luke's memorial of this voyage has more words in it than the Creation in Genesis, so it must be important! Paul began this trip as a prisoner of Rome, but in the end, he was leading everyone, including the Roman centurion, the captain of the ship, and a sailing master (*Called to Lead*, John MacArthur, p. 7).

Paul shows his passion through his commitment to the cause of witnessing. He does not have the title of a leader, but he continued to show leadership qualities throughout his mission for winning others to Christ. In Acts 21:13, he says, "What are you doing, weeping and breaking my heart? For I am ready not only to be bound, but even to die at Jerusalem for the name of the Lord Jesus." When one is willing to die for his cause, it is the ultimate example of passion.

In conclusion, as a leader, you must have a passion for leading people, or you will not survive. If you are currently a leader, you demonstrated that passion for getting you where you are. If your goal is to become a leader, I pray that this book can help you attain that goal. So come aboard this *Wave Making* vessel and bring your passion with you, the first item on your packing list. It doesn't weigh much, but it does carry a major influence on this *Wave Making* leadership voyage. Welcome aboard! Make Waves!

MAKING WAVES

The commitments or passion you choose make you!

They can *develop* you, or they can *destroy* you—regardless they will *define* you.

You become whatever you are committed to.

What will YOUR legacy be?

Figure out what you are passionate about. No passion results in unengaged boring people. Wave-making leadership is all about engaged, passionate people. Go and make your mark!

3

"ASSESSMENT" IS NOT A BAD WORD

Question everything!

What now? AWE—And What Else?

What is one thing I don't want to hear?

Good leaders look for answers, while leaders of significance look for better questions.

When the cook tastes the soup, that's formative assessment; when the customer tastes the soup, that's summative assessment.—Paul Black

You can teach a student a lesson for a day, but if you can teach him to learn by creating curiosity,

he will continue the learning process as long as he lives.—Clay P. Bedford

Never stop asking questions. Analyze every area of your organization. Always look at where you can improve your staff, facilities, and performance. Several years ago and until recently, a popular phrase for educators was "data-driven instruction." It has since become a negative phrase because of the amount of high-stakes testing and the amount of time devoted to preparing students to perform well on these tests. *High-stakes assessments became a perversion of its original intent!* The term *data* was mostly referring to those tests, benchmark tests, and other measurements committed to those assessments. I remember when I interviewed with several members of the selection committee for my last high school principal job. I was quick to answer, "We will use data-driven instruction," on a question dealing with pedagogy and how I measured teacher effectiveness. I recall the superintendent saying that a board member on the committee would hug me as a result of that answer.

However, we have come to realize that data can mean so many other ways to measure, assess, and analyze the plethora of information that we can gather as to how a child performs and even predict how well the student will achieve. Teachers do this all the time—maybe not in a formal written way, but by observation, student feedback, questioning, and examining how students work through problems, among other factors.

Whenever problems and issues arise in our day, obviously we begin to ask questions. However, I say we should ask questions before issues come up. If we are doing our job as leaders, we should continually ask questions. We should probably start with the five basic ones—*why, what, when, where,* and *who* (and I will add *how*). We should continually analyze our curriculum, personnel, assignments, budget, and more. I could go on for a while regarding what we need to conduct an analysis. There should be systems in place to make these evaluations. Our performance is often measured on how well we ask questions and analyze our campus, district, or organization. Maybe the best questions to ask are "What if...?" or "What are you wondering?"

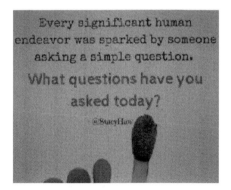

"Analyze your mistakes. You have already paid the tuition, you might as well get the lesson" —Tim Fargo, author of *Alphabet Success—Keeping it Simple. The Secret to Success*

My Twitter friend Stacey Hawthorne (@StacyHaw) tells me a story of one of her experiences in college.

A professor was able to ask the right questions and explain her answers in such a way that an epiphany would come to her, and the answer was there. He shared with her that the mark of a great teacher (leader) was not that they could solve all the problems, but that the teacher (leader) can help others see where they are stuck so that they can solve it themselves. Obviously, we need to be able to solve problems or issues when they arise, but it is also our job to enable others to solve their problems. She summed it up this way: leadership is the ability to problem-solve so that others think they could solve the problem all along.

My colleague Mike Ogg (@principalOgg—his dad was a great educational leader, as well) says,

---

Many would say that asking and analyzing is part of the reflection process. We, as leaders, should consistently reflect on our craft. Yet, the importance of reflection is to make sure that we ask and analyze. Both should be a part of reflecting.

You can ask all the questions you want, but if you are not analyzing what you are doing, then you might be asking the wrong questions. You and your crew can analyze programs and pull all the data to your heart's content. Yet, having the data will not help unless you ask the questions. Asking and analyzing is a continuous process that is always asking "what and why are we doing...?

As I am writing these words on asking questions, it is just as important to listen to the answers that are given. There are two of Covey's habits that come into play here: (1) be proactive, and (2) seek first to understand and then be understood. If we are to be proactive in our jobs, we will ask questions before problems arise. If we are asking the right questions from analyzing the situation, we can begin to arrive at the answer before a problem appears.

It is through questioning and analyzing that inventions are made, greatness appears, ideas are turned into realities, and plain is turned into amazing. You see, no one is born creative or great. Professional athletes and rock star musicians are not born; they are made over a long period. Leaders are not born; they are made. In many books I have read about people who are superstars in their field, I learned that it took preparation, trial and error, and failing over and over, totaling about

10,000 hours of trials, practicing, and analyzing their performance before greatness finally happened. They did not stop once they achieved greatness; they continued this regimen.

I was fortunate to reach my boyhood dream of playing in the National Football League. I started playing organized football in the fourth grade when I was ten-years-old. I began to practice punting then. My father knew an industrial psychologist, Al Chapman, who had done research on the skill/art of punting a football. As a result, Dr. Chapman would periodically come for what he referred to as "tune-ups" for me. He would watch me and, after each punt, would advise me on what I did right and wrong. These sessions would last about thirty to forty-five minutes. About 90 percent of the time, he would toss me the ball, and I would merely punt it back to him. This was so frustrating to me because I wanted to go full speed and see how far, how high I could punt it. Then the last few minutes, he would allow me to punt away. Little did I know the science behind this type of practice. Both my parents would often ask, "Have you punted today?" I loved punting, but I also loved to play basketball, baseball, and golf, as well as skateboard. I was a normal boy wanting to do everything. I could do/play all those things, but they wanted me to practice my punting before/after those activities. My point? After I read several books on what it took to reach a world-class skill, I found a simple formula for what it took to reach the top in any endeavor. The formula is simple. Execution of that formula is what separates the good from the great! It is the following:

$$\text{deep practice } x \text{ 10,000 hours} = \text{world class skill}$$

The book that describes this in detail is *The Talent Code* by Daniel Coyle, a great book for any coach, teacher, or leader, as it describes what it takes to reach the pinnacle in any field. Gladwell's book, *Outliers,* also speaks to the 10,000 hours needed to achieve mastery or elite status.

I loved to practice. I know, kinda weird. I believe this to be true of all who reach mastery or world-class. Fortunately, I had a Dr. Chapman and a father who would watch me, correct me, ask me questions after each punt, encourage me, and help me set goals to work and reach for and eventually compete at the highest level. I estimate I trained or deep practiced over 10,000 hours by the time I reached the NFL. When I go to a stadium to watch an NFL game, I am in awe that I was once one of those guys.

I share this story with you so that you can see that it takes hours, assessment, work, and sacrifice to move from average or very good to elite. Many think that elite athletes, musicians, performers, artists, or leaders have some kind of natural skill or ability. These natural skills or abilities are a result of thousands of hours of deep practice or reflection of performance and seeking to achieve perfection. I am saying it is not easy to be really good. It takes years of trial and error, taking risks, and failing before finally, things start to come together.

You see, if it were easy or just a matter of reading a few books, going to a few conferences, and listening to a few elite performers in your field, there would be hundreds of thousands of world-class leaders. However, we all know that there are only a few who have reached the top of their profession.

I know that we all want to have elite schools, districts, and organizations. I am not saying it would take ten thousand hours to achieve that. What I am saying is that it takes trials, practice, questions, and analysis before it happens.

One of the practices I have learned and use to this day comes from the legendary author and motivator, Zig Ziglar. He shared that any time he read a book, it was nonfiction, motivating, biographies of great people, and/or self-improvement. I began using that choice of reading after a couple of years of teaching and after training to teach his course. As a result, I have a library of books to which I can continually refer. I highlight, mark, and tab so it is much easier for me to find an idea, reference, or quote that I can apply for a situation. At one point, I committed to turning off the TV at 9:00 p.m. and read until bedtime, and found that I was able to read about two books a month.

Sometimes even when you are asking, analyzing, practicing, and reading, problems will come, and greatness will not always be achieved. However, I am saying that if we continually ask questions and analyze our school, district, organization, and selves, we will get closer to greatness than if we did not commit to those actions.

As you read books, listen to speakers, and visit exemplary schools or organizations, all this information is getting stored in your mind. As I read, I always analyze ways I can apply the information that I am reading either to myself or to my school or district.

You will be surprised when some idea, answer, practice, or system comes to mind as a result of the data/input that you continually place in your brain. I have heard or read that the unconscious mind has a perfect memory. I am still amazed when people come to me after a presentation or follow me on Twitter and tell me I have inspired them. I truly do not think I am inspirational. To me, it is just ideas and words coming from me as a result of years of reading, listening to recordings of great people, and going to conferences. I just share my experiences! I am not sure I have (or had) any original idea. I just cultivate or tweak what I have already seen, read, or heard.

Please understand that committing to doing all the things I just talked about not only can make you a better leader, but also a better, more rounded individual.

As I think about bringing this chapter to a close, I think about assessment and pirates, and how they relate.

What? Wait, what?

Do these two words belong in the same book, let alone in the same chapter? I have given you a little information about pirates and how I perceived that they practiced the attributes of wave-making leadership. However, you don't have to think too much to realize that pirates were probably fairly good at analyzing their voyages, strategies, crew, and how to handle the supplies and booty that they plundered.

Now let me turn to the Original *Wave-Maker*, Paul. We pick up in the middle of the voyage to Rome as Paul begins to assert himself as one who knows how to handle rough seas (some scholars even say it was close to a hurricane) and navigate through unknown waters. Paul had predicted that a storm would ensue, and advised the Roman leaders not to continue the voyage while anchored at Fair Havens. As the storm became more violent, the Roman sailors began to panic. Even the most seasoned sailor fears getting caught in a sea that is full of twenty-foot waves and salty seawater splashing in the boat, having to fight to survive! It is at this point that Paul became the leader of the ship. He assured them that there would be no loss of life, but they would eventually lose the ship. Paul confidently said to the whole crew,

> For this very night an angel of the God to whom I belong and whom I serve stood before me, saying, "Do not be afraid, Paul; you must stand before Caesar; and behold, God has granted you all those who are sailing with you," therefore, keep up your courage, men, for I believe God, that it will turn out exactly as I have been told. But we must run aground on a certain island."
> (Acts 27: 22–26)

Paul was not just any kind of leader—he became a *fearless* leader. He was able to accomplish this because he knew Who controlled the seas. Also, he had a relationship with the Creator of those seas. He was able to analyze the problem and even predict the outcome because of that relationship with God. From this point in the voyage, Paul was looked upon as the leader from everyone on the ship, including the Roman crew sailing the ship.

We are getting close to complete our packing for our voyage. Analysis must be brought on board, for it is through assessment that we understand where we are and where we want to go. It can assist us in our performance of our organization, personnel, and facilities. As Dr. Wendell Brown, AVID Central Division Director, says, "the power is in the refinement." Assessment may be quite heavy, but surely a necessity for our quest of leadership excellence. Do not will yourself to achieve, but ask your way to success.

MAKING WAVES

"Avoid the dreaded Ttwwadi (That's The Way We've Always Done It)"—Amy Mayer @friEDTechnology

---

I believe this may be *the* biggest hindrance to change in education today.

Keep a journal. What did I accomplish today? What were my struggles? Your thoughts are clarified as they are written.

Analyze the issues that cross your desk.

- Is this a problem to be solved, or tension to be managed?
- Is this MY problem?
- Just how big is this problem?

4

YOU MUST HAVE PERSEVERANCE!

I'm convinced that about half of what separates successful leaders from the non-successful ones is pure perseverance. —Steve Jobs

Perseverance is the hard work you do after you get tired of doing the hard work you already did. —Newt Gingrich

Blessed is the one who perseveres under trial, having stood the test, that person will receive the crown of life that the Lord has promised to those who love Him.—James 1:12

Press on. Nothing in the world can take the place of persistence. Talent will not; nothing is more common than unsuccessful (people) with talent. Genius will not; the world is full of educated derelicts. Persistence and determination alone are omnipotent.—Ray Kroc

Grit: a combination of passion and perseverance for a singularly important goal—is the hallmark of high achievers in every domain.—Angela Duckworth

Leadership has no period—only commas and question marks; it is never-ending.

Whenever I hear the word *perseverance*, it is usually not in a positive context. It is usually associated with pain, obstacles, problems, valleys—I could probably fill the page with the words that I usually associate with perseverance. However, if you look it up in the dictionary, you will find these synonyms: *doggedness*, *steadfastness*, *persistence*, *tenacity*; these words are more on a positive slant.

Always remember that someone else has been dealt worse cards than you and is winning. Keep playing your cards and embrace them, and play them the best you can. Perseverance is a word that many of us will use throughout our leadership careers.

Angela Duckworth, in her book entitled *Grit — The Power of Perseverance and Passion,* wrote about the importance of perseverance. However, she added later in her book that other attributes made a successful person (some of which I outline in this book). Educational neuroscience research says that as students try, then fail, then keep trying until they can "get it," deeper learning happens.

During my tenure as principal in elementary and two high schools and finally as superintendent, there were not many times when people would make an appointment to see me to say, "Hal, I just came to tell you what a good job you have been doing..." Interestingly, I had many of those after I announced my resignation. I finally came to the conclusion that it is the "nature of the beast."

Steve Jobs once said, "I'm convinced that about half of what separates the successful entrepreneurs from the non-successful ones is pure perseverance." You can substitute *leaders* in place of *entrepreneurs* in that statement. Thomas Edison said, "Many of life's failures are people who did not realize how close they were to success when they gave up." Perseverance is a key attribute for all leaders to possess. Things will go wrong, but you have to know that you made the decision for the right reason.

Leaders cannot be timid, and they certainly cannot be weak. We as people grow the most during turbulent times. Robin

Williams said, "You will have bad times, but they will always wake you up to the stuff you weren't paying attention to." There are times that you may feel like you are pretty beat-up. However, take comfort in that we all feel that way at times. You were chosen to be a leader, and those who chose you saw that you could handle tough situations.

One Thursday when I was a high school principal, a student-athlete of mine died during the athletic period in the middle of the day. It was one of the saddest and most challenging days of my leadership. I witnessed coaches using CPR on him, and I watched as the paramedics placed paddles on him to shock his heart back to beating again. I had to get on the PA system to announce to my students that one of their classmates had passed away. I was the person that his mother sought to find out how her son is doing. Yes, I had to tell her that he did not make it.

The following morning, I met with my faculty to try to plan how to handle the grief that our students were experiencing. We called neighboring schools to send their counselors to our campus to be on standby as needed for our kids. I had them positioned throughout the building so they could assess and counsel our students. I tried my best to convey to my teachers that there was "no right way" to grieve—only that they could count on not covering a whole lot of curriculum that day. They could teach some lessons, but most importantly, they needed to have a listening and caring ear and maybe a shoulder to cry on. I spent the whole day in the halls talking to kids and giving hugs. My students and I shed many tears that day. I had another faculty meeting that afternoon to debrief and to thank them for the job that everyone did. The entire faculty exhibited love, care, compassion—I could go on and on about how admirably they conducted themselves.

The funeral was the following Thursday at 1:00 p.m., the same day the state-mandated exit math exam was to be administered to 11th graders, who had to pass this test to graduate. I met with the entire junior class in the auditorium on Monday. I could not have asked for a more engaged group of change-makers. I tried my best to convey how hard it was on them and that I could only imagine what emotions they were feeling. At the same time, I had to encourage them to try their best to succeed on their test. Scores for our school were the furthest from my mind. I wanted what was best for them, and that was for them to pass to be able to graduate. I was proud of my students, who seemed to receive my comments well.

On that Thursday, our students performed admirably. That morning, the student's mother asked me to say a few words at the funeral. Oh my! I started to write some words, but ultimately I was led to just stand and share what a special student he was, how popular he was among his classmates, and that he seemed to always have a smile on his face.

The following Thursday, my choir director was carried away on a Life Flight helicopter after he suffered a heart attack. Thankfully, he survived and was even able to finish the year. I didn't want to go to school on the following Thursday!

Years later, I vividly recall how our faculty, staff, students, and community bonded through those weeks. It was really beautiful to see rainbows after the storm. During those three weeks, I learned more about leadership than several books could teach me. I tried to be empathetic to everyone—teachers, support staff, and most of all, my students. I learned that I had to be strong in front of my faculty, my students, and my community. No matter how I was feeling, I had to be decisive, show resilience, and have confidence in my words. I tried to remember what I said after the faculty and student meetings I conducted. For the life of me, I could not remember many details. I do know that my prayers were answered and God provided me with the words to say.

There was another issue that I had to deal with as a high-school principal. Those of you who are high school principals, you have probably dealt with class rank, National Honor Society, cheerleaders, and more. This particular issue concerned a tie for salutatorian. Thank goodness we had an excellent policy on tie-breaking in place. As my senior counselor and I looked at the policy, we looked at the steps to break the tie. The first was the highest number of AP/honor courses—both had the same. The second was the highest numerical grade average in AP/honors courses—both had the same! I began to get nervous. The third was the highest numerical grade average in all classes. The tie was broken! One actually had a 94 average, while the other had a 93 average in one class. Oh my! My superintendent insisted that I break the tie, so it was my job to call the girls in my office to break the news. I also needed to meet with the parents to share how our policy was worded. Oh, I forgot to mention—they were twin sisters!

As I shared the news, both girls began to cry, even as I was tearing up. The one ranked third choked out these words, which broke my heart, "I have always been the dumb one!" I had to gather myself, I went to hug her, and we just had a good cry for a few minutes. As they walked down the hallway together, an idea hit me! I called them back to my office and asked, "What if you both gave the salutatory address?" They beamed, and one of them said, "Mr. Roberts, don't tell our parents! We want to surprise them on graduation night! That is an awesome idea." On graduation night, as I announced for the salutatorian to come to the stage, I watched their parents, who began to cry while smiling proudly. It was a special time that I will always remember.

For those of you who are trying for that "next rung on the

ladder" of leadership —persevere. I probably submitted dozens of applications for each job that I applied. There were even years between the first application and finally achieving my next goal. Continue to network, seek guidance, and keep at it. Your time to shine will come.

As a leader, it is not *if*, but *when* trials and challenges come. The test of a great leader is how he responds to the storms that sometimes come out of nowhere. A trusted friend of mine once told me that the best a leader can expect is 80 percent support. I am not sure if that is researched-based, but I think it is fairly accurate.

Often, leaders have someone second-guessing or maybe even trying to undermine the vision they have for the organization. I must stress that you strive for strength in *adversity* and how to overcome it. This is one of the most valuable lessons that one learns in athletics. I honestly don't think students can learn this in the classroom. Through losses, injuries, not making the starting lineup, missing a game-winning basket, striking out with runners on base—the experiences are almost endless. Sometimes it is simply going through two-a-days in August that develops one's perseverance!

The apostle Paul certainly exhibited perseverance. He was beaten, stoned, shipwrecked three times, imprisoned, hungered (this is real hunger!) and spent a night and day in the open sea alone. In Acts 27, during Paul's voyage to Rome, he suffered a time of rough seas and bad weather. Verses 7–8 state, "When we had sailed slowly for a good many days, and with difficulty had arrived off Cnidus, since the wind did not permit us to go farther, we sailed under the shelter of Crete, off Salmone; and with difficulty sailing past it we came to a place called Fair Havens, near which was the city of Lasea."

The voyage was long and treacherous. Paul was beginning to gain trust among the Roman centurion guarding him, along with most of the rest of the crew. You should understand Paul was beginning to assist the captain and first mate in navigating the ship through rough waters and increasingly intense strong winds. Paul was patient as he persevered until his time to lead came.

In Romans, Paul says this about perseverance:

Therefore, having been justified by faith, we have peace with God through our Lord Jesus Christ, through whom also we have obtained our introduction by faith into this grace in which we stand; and we exult in hope of the glory of God. And not only this, but we also exult in our tribulations, knowing that tribulation brings about perseverance; and perseverance, proven character; and proven character, hope; and hope does not disappoint, because the love of God has been poured out within our hearts through the Holy Spirit who was given to us. (Rom. 5: 1–5)

My Twitter friend Mandy Johnson, (@DrJohnsonEDU) shares this about perseverance:

Don't settle for easy because you can. Instead, find your mountains and reach the top of them." It's at the pinnacle that you'll see and experience a vast amount of beauty. This type of beauty is indescribable. I hope each child reaches this pinnacle at some point before they graduate. If we can do this, our students will never want to stop feeling what it is like at the top. Perseverance is all about what we do to reach the summit.

From a faith-based standpoint, why should we try? Why should we persevere? Because He would want nothing less from us.

There is a song called the "MLK Song," written by Patty Griffin in 2007. It's a gorgeous song with a precious message—maybe one of the most inspirational songs I've heard. Griffin lyrically shares King's tired and weary journey in this world as he strives to bring about a peaceful change. King experienced a conglomeration of feelings, which stemmed from being loved, hated, empowered, insulted, saddened, and more. The road to the mountain God had called him to move was not an easy one, to say the least. At times, King could see the stretch as promising, while other times, he felt overwhelmed. When he was ready to give in, God was there to catch him and give him rest. Persevering is not about giving it all you got until you tire through complete exhaustion. Perseverance is giving it your best with the talents God has given you. If He asks you to go there, He will bring you to the finish line in some way or another. However, it is also about the journey...not the end that matters. People will watch you along the way. A part of the perseverance factor is being transparent. Falling is a natural process of learning. Without falls, learning does not occur. Others do not want to see a perfect march to any mountain. How intimidating is that? Great leaders inspire, not intimidate! People need to see you fall, stand up, brush yourself off, smile, continue, and share what you learned along the way.

For me, my journey has been built from so many broken roads that I've lost count at this point. At the intersection of these roads, I have found pivotal points. What do I do at these crossroads? I pray! I pray! I pray! Then, I pray again. I have learned that there will be days when I don't see the sun or even glimpses of it. I have also learned to relax because there are always better days ahead.

No, I have not always possessed leadership traits, as many people do. My leadership abilities were born from a series of God-given experiences, which were not very pleasant I might add. I am very passionate about my calling, and could not be happier in the profession God chose for me. If He calls you to it, then go to the mountain and make it yours. Remember...no matter the journey, always choose joy and persevere.

Dabo Swinney, head coach of National Champions Clemson Tigers says, "we are made for the climb, the journey, the grind, the relationships along the way, the struggles. Those mountaintop experiences are great, but life is about having joy in the journey..."

As we continue our voyage of leadership, perseverance is a priority to carry with you, perhaps a little heavier than passion. It is only one of many of the necessities for our journey. As we travel these ocean seas, we have to be ready for storms and turbulence. Together we will reach our destination.

MAKING WAVES

Every *Wave-Making* ship must be prepared to ride out gales and storms at sea. The pirate Edward Low was heading for the Leeward Islands in a brigantine when a hurricane swept across his path. Mountainous waves threatened to overcome him; for hours, he worked the pumps used to bail water. He debated whether to cut away the masts but, decided against this and instead rigged preventer shrouds to secure the main-mast and lay upon the other tack, till the storm was over.

Edward Low and his crew of wave-makers persevered in the storm. He showed leadership in his decisions during rough waters and was able to make it to shore.

5

DRENCH YOURSELF IN EVERY ASPECT OF YOUR JOB

The moment when you finally see what lies beneath the surface...you realize how you had been missing out on the whole point of the ocean.

Unless you are willing to drench yourself in your work beyond the capacity of the average man, you are just not cut for positions at the top.—J. C. Penney

Drench your staff in "your way" of doing things. Southwest Airlines has four standards in the

Southwest way—positively outrageous customer service, warrior spirit, fun-loving attitude, and leading from a servant heart.

Total immersion in life offers the best classroom for learning to love.—Leo Buscaglia

From a poker phrase, be "all in!"

When I hear the word *drench*, I think of the TV show *Undercover Boss*, where CEOs disguise themselves and go "undercover" to discover issues in their business. They always seem to find "hidden" talented workers who have heart-wrenching stories. The CEO eventually reveals his true identity and rewards them for jobs well done. Then I wonder, why did it take a reality TV show for them to conduct these sessions or visits?

During my presentation, I show a person diving into water to see what the ocean is all about. You have to get below the surface or immerse yourself in the sea before you can learn about the waters. I like to give the illustration of four different kinds of people (maybe leaders): (1) those who are in the boat looking out at the waters, (2) those who are actively water-skiing, (3) those who are snorkeling and able to see underneath the surface of the water, and (4) finally those who are scuba diving and able to experience the wonders of the sea. Which one are you?

I love the title of one of Harvey MacKay's books, *Swim with the Sharks Without Being Eaten Alive*. It is not about literally swimming with sharks, but actually a sales book with a plethora of leadership suggestions in it. As leaders, we have to be pretty good salespeople, able to "sell" our vision to our stakeholders. But before we talk about our vision, we must be in the perpetual discovery of our organization. Whenever I was hired for a new position, I would first obtain a copy of the most current yearbook and begin to place names with faces. We all know the power of calling someone by name!

One of my Twitter friends, Bethany Hill, the principal/lead learner at Central Cabot Elementary School in Arkansas and Bammy Award Nominee, places a sign on her office door as she leaves to visit classrooms, *"Out for a 'joy' ride."* She knows the value of leaving her office to experience her entire campus. I actually had to schedule my time out of my office. If I didn't, I would get stuck in my office. I left my office to get into the halls, cafeteria, fields, courts, and music halls. I was reminded that this is the reason I do what I do.

My colleague and vital member of my PLN, Jay Posick (@posickj), writes,

---

Immersion into a school environment is vital for the success of a school. If the leader is not immersed in the activities and content of the campus and does not show concern for all that occurs, the school will have rough sailing. Leaders need to show an interest and be the "head cheerleader" for the students and staff. This is the only way that he can have a pulse on the organization.

I had a Facebook post shared with me recently about Dr. Drew Watkins, superintendent of Prosper Independent School District (ISD) in Texas. I found out from teachers that he writes a personal note of congratulations to every graduating senior, 403 this past year. It was asked how he learns about each student. Teachers said he knows them. He is in the schools all the time, not in his office. He loves the students, and they love him back.

Availability and being seen is the best way to build relationships—the primary way to evaluate/assess your staff, programs, and facilities. If you put a value on creating relationships, you will not choose to stay in your office, where it is very difficult to evaluate any area of your supervision.

When I was hired as superintendent, my school board charged me to create/build a high school. I had been fortunate to serve as principal in two high schools and athletic director in another. As a result, I knew most of what went on in a high school and what it took to create one. But when we began to create a school, I had to totally immerse myself in policy, handbooks, curriculum, programs, budget, and more to truly understand what made a high school. Three years later, the first graduating class walked across the stage.

We as leaders must go beyond simply immersing ourselves in our campus or district—we also must engage in our community. You can do this in many ways. You can join service organizations or make yourself visible in community events. In 2000, I felt fortunate to be a part and speak at a Martin Luther King Jr. celebration in a community where I served as high school principal and lived. I was completely out of my comfort zone, but I did so gladly, as it was a way to avail myself in another part of the community. I was a member of Lions Club in one city, had been asked to teach Sunday school in four different churches, and also served as a deacon. These are several examples of immersing yourself in the community where you work.

I attended a conference recently, listening to Angela Maiers give her presentation, "Mattering IS the Agenda," and she asked Todd Nesloney, principal of an elementary school in Navasota, Texas, to give an example of getting involved in his community. He and his faculty and staff went to several apartment complexes, took a huge grill, and cooked and served hotdogs with fixings to the community. When he was asked why he was doing this, he replied, "It's because we love you and wanted to find a way to serve you and a way for you to ask us anything about our school or district." What an amazing way to show his community that his faculty cared for their community! If you feed them, they will come. (Those are my words, but I think it works.)

In my job as superintendent, every morning and afternoon, I would stand at my carpool lane greeting change-makers, waving and speaking to parents as they dropped off or picked up their babies. (They are all babies, no matter what age/grade to their parents.) This was a great way to begin and end my day, even though I was at school before and after carpool. This hour of my day was well worth the investment of my time. It really was an investment because it paid dividends. I did not do it for that reason, but because I wanted them to know I cared, and it allowed me to demonstrate that every kid matters every day.

It is very simple to see how Paul was immersed in his voyage. He did not accept his lot of being a prisoner, but chose instead to use this time to show his love and expertise in the navigation to the men who were holding him captive. I believe love is not a feeling or emotion, but a choice. Paul chose to love his captors, and in turn, they began to trust and respect him. Eventually, there were 276 men on this voyage, including prisoners (in addition to Paul), the centurion, and other Romans who were tasked with running, navigating, and feeding all of these men, plus whoever else was needed for this mission. Paul took this opportunity (he turns every encounter into an opportunity) to gain trust and respect during the most tempestuous part of the voyage. He didn't do this by feeling sorry for himself as a prisoner. Instead, he got out and immersed himself with everyone on board.

The only way to know your faculty is by continuously going into their world. When it comes to programs, we all know, "it is all personnel." That phrase was coined and often used by one of my mentors, Dick Walton, now retired superintendent of Bay City ISD in Bay City, Texas. He also reminded us all to "do the right things for the right reasons." As school leaders, we are charged to assign personnel to the right position. The only good way of appointing someone to a position is to fully know her. This is achieved by immersing yourself in the culture of your campus or district.

When you practice "swimming" with your students, faculty, staff, and community, they get to see the real you. In scripture, the word *abide* comes to mind when I think of drenching. When it is mentioned, it is always in reference to a very close relationship to whoever is mentioned next. So it should be our goal to abide with all of our stakeholders both inside our building or district, as well as our community. I will have to say that drenching takes quite a bit of effort on your part. You will have to spend time, and it will never end, not even when you go to the grocery store or the mall in your community.

Drenching is a pretty heavy item to carry on our voyage of *Wave Making* leadership. However, we are not like the airlines, and you can bring as much cargo as you need. This payload cannot buy you anything at the store, but it can purchase a legacy that will live long after you leave your district. A true leader's measure is not by the number of followers he has, but the number of leaders he makes. Make sure you pack drenching for this long voyage. This is the heaviest piece at this point, but well worth the load. Let's stay the course on our expedition as we sail together on the high seas.

MAKING WAVES

If I had to define leadership in one word, it would be influence. If you lose your influence, you cannot and will not lead. You cannot influence in your office. You must immerse yourself in your dominion.

6

BUILD SAFE & HEALTHY RELATIONSHIPS

Busyness is the greatest enemy of relationships.

All relationships go through hell, real relationships get through it.—The Love Bits

To inspire meaningful change, you must first make a connection to the heart before you make a connection to the mind.

We must heal the soul before we can move to the academic component. The way to heal the soul is through intentional relationships and authentic love.

Relationships are still the killer app for learning and leading.

School (life) - relationships = 0 or nothing

Time (our most precious asset) + investment (effort) = love (relationships)

People will do most anything for leaders they know, like, admire, & trust.

We are genetically and environmentally social creatures. We seek relationships. We want to belong.

Leadership is all about inspiring people to follow. We have to remember, leaders lead people. It is always about the people you lead. It is not about the vision, the plan, the program; it is about your people. As a result, everything depends on the leader's ability to relate to her staff. Developing healthy, positive relationships may be the most important attribute or skill a leader can possess. No matter what book I have read, leader I have talked with, or Twitter chat I have participated in, developing relationships continues to rise to the top of the priority list. Virtually all the educational neuroscience books I have read support this as well.

Fearless and courageous leaders lead from their heart and not from hurt and fear. As I have personally experienced and researched more than 20 leaderships books, I have come to the conclusion that great leaders are vulnerable and humble. You see when you exhibit both of these, you draw yourself to the people that follow you. As Brené Brown says in her book *Dare to Lead*, "You can't get to courage without rumbling with vulnerability. Embrace the suck." We cannot be daring, courageous, fearless, or Wave-Making without embracing vulnerability. This connects us to our followers. So we must take off the armor that protects us from "rumbling with vulnerability." Rumbling with vulnerability is making tough calls, having hard conversations, and taking risks. As you do all of these, your followers gain trust and respect that attracts them to you in a more personal way.

The greatest movie of all time, *The Wizard of Oz*, illustrates a perfect story of creating healthy/positive relationships. It also shows the results of such relationships and collaboration. Dorothy begins her journey after a very unfortunate accident, alone until she meets her three future friends and crew. They not only help her get to the Emerald City, but also to meet the great and powerful Oz and ultimately defeat her enemy. It is through her building relationships that they were able to follow the yellow brick road to find the wizard. The final results showed her and her crew's resolve in overcoming obstacles and achieving her vision of finding her way home. We can learn a lot from Dorothy with how she encourages, inspires, motivates, loves, supports, protects, and ultimately shows the Tin Man, the Cowardly Lion, and the Scarecrow that they matter.

Through my research, I have found that happiness has three fundamental components: Relationships/Belonging, Freedom/Autonomy, and Meaningful Work/Mastery. You can use these three components in both students and staff. It all begins relationships.

I show a video in my presentations regarding relationships and social media. It alleges that social media is actually an "antisocial" media tool. It illustrates how a device can get in the way of a true, personal relationship. Regardless of how you feel about social media, realize this: social media, more specifically Twitter, is a game-changer for us in education. You can make valuable relationships and obtain great professional development on demand—just look for it. As you can see from reading, I have gleaned a plethora of wisdom, inspiration, and knowledge from the educators on Twitter.

People need to know that you will be for them even if they make a mistake. Please understand: they will actually perform better knowing that you are there when they fail. They know if they do make a mistake, you will be there to help them learn from it, support them, and not punish them. Leaders lead people who work in the organization. Remember, it is the people, not the organization, in whom you invest your time. In the end, that investment will pay off.

Angela Maiers once tweeted me by saying, "We MUST secure the heart or we don't have a shot at the brain!" as a response to Mandy Johnson's (@DrJohnsonEDU) tweet: "My new quote...Teaching is total heart work." This applies to leadership as well. I have made another friend, Kate Lindquist, an art educator, and I love her tag: @heARTISTat-WORK. It kind of goes along with what Mandy says.

Leading any organization is like walking on a tightrope—the tightrope of when to use power and when not to, as well as realizing that when you use power, you lose power. You rarely get immediate feedback on the success or failure of your leadership. Relationships can serve as a "place to fall." They will be there during your tough times and good times. They will encourage you in your valleys and be your best cheerleader during the good times.

If someone were to ask you, "what do you do all day?" what is your answer? If it is to go to meetings and solve conflicts, then you are missing the most important attribute of a leader—that you should spend most of your day developing positive relationships.

In Malcolm Gladwell's book *Outliers*, he wrote in the first chapter about a community in Roseto, Pennsylvania—a community of European immigrants. Physicians studied

Rosetans because their average life span was 30 to 40 percent longer than any other neighboring town or in the United States. The Rosetans virtually eliminated heart attacks as a cause of death. The more the physicians studied, the more perplexed they were. It was not their diet, because many were obese and many smoked heavily. They didn't exercise any more than other people. They finally determined that the Rosetans just died of old age. What the researchers eventually discovered about the Rosetans' longevity was their sense of community that increased their life-span. They placed a premium on family and friendships. They valued and practiced nurturing relationships!

The brain is social. It looks for ways to develop relationships. Neuroscience says that this is probably the most important piece of learning. My friend Julie Adams (@adamsteaching) writes in her book *Game Changers: 7 Instructional Practices That Catapult Student Achievement* (a great book for a book study), "Optimal brain engagement occurs when there is a positive emotional connection between the student and teacher. Relationships, relationships, relationships. It makes a considerable difference in students' learning potential." I asked her once about relationships, and she told me, "They may be *the* most important factor of a productive learning environment."

Furthermore, in *Leading with the Brain in Mind* by Dickman, Stanford-Blair, and Rosati-Bojar, the authors state, "The brain both expects and depends on the provocation of social experience to do its job...Social experience then, is the great provocateur of thinking and learning." The point I am trying to make is this: as a leader, you must begin your vision for the organization with developing and nurturing positive relationships. This takes a great amount of time and effort on your part, but it will pay huge dividends in everything that you will ever do in leadership. Just as it is important for teachers to work on this every day to enhance student learning, we, as leaders, must work on this daily. You should strive to develop relationships with your community, as well.

In a previous chapter on immersion, I gave some examples of starting relationships. The only way to develop relationships is to get out of your office. As you leave your office, you immediately become more accessible. There is no longer a desk or a door that separates you from your stakeholders. Usually, you are more at ease and, most likely, will be a little more open to conversations. You are now in an environment where people feel more at ease, as well. Therefore, you can more easily develop and cultivate positive, healthy relationships. I have found that your faculty and staff love to see you out of your office. They usually invite you into their classroom or area. Not only does this help build a relationship with your faculty, but it also enhances your relationships with your change-makers.

All leaders, at some point, must have tough conversations. Do not shy away from difficult conversations. These types of discussions, when you tackle them together, will improve your brain and probably improve your relationships. Sometimes, you should ask the tough questions. When I was a superintendent, I once asked a teacher, "Do you feel supported?" Her response was a little more than I bargained for, but I also gained a trusted crew member. She realized that I cared after that conversation and that she could count on honest conversations in the future, as well as my support for her. These kinds of questions can sometimes shed light on a blind spot or two.

When it comes to relationships, perhaps one of the top priorities is to develop an inner circle. You do not need over four or five in your circle, including yourself. Some leadership books I have read say that there can be up to eight or ten in the inner circle. With more than four or five, there are too many opinions that can cloud the brainstorming. These are part of your leadership crew. Do not let titles (i.e., Assistant Principal) determine your choice—consider including a teacher in that inner circle.

Choose your inner circle carefully. Again, no matter how large your organization is, your circle should not have more than four or five. Please understand it is important to have members who know different areas of your organization.

The inner circle should take some time to assemble. These

members should have a servant attitude. Not necessarily a servant to the leader, but to the people of the organization. The top priority for this circle of professionals is to trust each other implicitly and be loyal to each other. When this group discusses strategy, personnel, policy, or anything of significance, it should be understood that whatever is talked about stays within the circle. Another understanding is that anyone can disagree or question and is even encouraged to do so; however, once a decision is made, all are on on-board and moving forward without looking back. This group should be a picture of teamwork and efficiency.

A word of caution: you should choose your inner circle, not inherit it. I should also caution to not consider experience as a qualification. Some of my most loyal and valuable circle members had no experience in administration. I should also mention that some of my most fruitful decisions came in a casual, informal gathering of my inner circle. This was because we often asked, "What if?" and would come up with some great ideas.

The main attribute of healthy, positive relationships is loyalty. One cannot build a relationship if there is no loyalty. This takes time, effort, and honesty to develop loyalty among your relationships. It takes honest concern, answers, and empathy when dealing with your staff, parents, and community. Sometimes I just wanted to "take time off and not be on," but that is not what I signed up for, and neither have you if you want to be a successful leader. You see, when at church, the grocery store, or the mall, when people see you, they see the leader of their campus or district, so you must continue to serve in that role. It is at these times that those relationships are truly nurtured, so take advantage of those opportunities.

I refer you to the chapter on passion. If you exhibit passion for your position of leadership, you will thrive in this area. You will not see it as a nuisance, but a chance to nurture or build more relationships. Creating and nurturing relationships is a good way to ensure a healthy culture. As you build positive, sincere relationships in your organization, you begin to build a healthy culture. As your people get to know you and you them, this builds bridges of trust. I will expound on trust in a later chapter.

I choose to believe we were created for relationships. Neuroscience also supports this. To draw inspiration from my faith, at the beginning of time, man craved a relationship. We were created to have relationships, first with God and later with each other. God created a man, then saw that he needed more on earth than just animals. God said, "I can do better than that!" (after looking at the man). So from the man's rib (as he had a spare rib!), God created a woman (a prime rib!). Now the story goes that the woman was wandering around and saw the tree of Knowledge of Good and Evil. Then there was the serpent who was very conniving and pleasing to the eye. The serpent persuaded her to eat the fruit of the tree of knowledge of good and evil, even though she knew she was not to eat of it. As a result, she and Adam hid from God. So God called out to Adam, "Oh, Adam, where are you?" Adam responded, "We are hiding since we are naked!" Now God was getting a little frustrated at this, since before they were naked and not ashamed. So he asked Adam, "Who told you that you were naked?" Adam responded, "Well, that woman that you sent me," pointing at Eve. Adam tried not to be accountable. Then God looked to Eve and asked the same, "Who told you?" Eve then responded, "Well, that serpent." Then God angrily looked at the serpent and put a curse on him, and of course, the serpent didn't have a leg to stand on. Now that is Hal's Revised Version (HRV), so that may not be exactly as it is written in the Bible, but you get the gist.

When Paul was taken as prisoner on the voyage to Rome, there were two friends of Paul who accompanied him. Now I don't know about you, but if a friend asked me to join him on a prison boat, I am not so sure I would jump at the chance. However, Luke (the author of Acts) and Aristarchus (interestingly his name meant "best leader") accompanied him on this journey. Now, this speaks volumes of how Paul developed relationships. These two men sacrificed their freedom to join Paul. Not only did he have deep relationships with a few men, but also with entire churches. You can see the intimacy of Paul and the churches that he started and led from the letters he wrote to them.

The best example of his loyalty, devotion, and passion is his letters to the church at Corinth. Loyalty is right up there with trust, and loyalty works both ways. Paul was loyal to the Corinthian church. Heck, 1 Corinthian 13 is often used in weddings as it states the characteristics of love. Throughout this letter, he showed compassion, empathy, and love for his church. If you, as a leader, can show these traits or principles that Paul displayed in the Corinthian letters, you will be an exemplary leader.

We are on our way of packing for our compelling journey of leadership. Now we must pack relationships in our trunk. This piece is not as heavy as some others, but it is the most important, so make plenty of room. Relationship building should be listed as your top priority when leading any group of people.

MAKING WAVES

Geronimo, the leader of the Apache Nation, is a perfect example of building relationships. Geronimo was a great leader. We can learn a great amount of what it takes by reading *Geronimo: Leadership Strategies of the American Warrior* by Mike Leach and Buddy Levy, the book from where my information on Geronimo originates.

Geronimo believed that if you are loyal to your people, they will be loyal to you. He also believed that you should be utterly devoted to your people. He developed the ability to connect with his warriors. Geronimo thought developing positive relationships was a very important attribute as a leader.

7

THERE IS NO SUCH THING AS A MINOR LAPSE OF INTEGRITY

If you value your integrity, then be prepared to take a beating from those who have none.—Lars Lau Thygesen

Integrity is choosing courage over comfort; choosing what is right over what is fun, fast, or easy; and choosing to practice our values rather than simply professing them.—Brené Brown

Listen with curiosity. Speak with honesty. Act with integrity.—Roy Bennet

No matter how educated, talented, rich, or cool

you are, how you treat people ultimately tells all. Integrity is everything.

Live in such a way that is if somebody spoke badly of you, no one would believe it.

Integrity takes time to build and acquire, but only a moment to lose. At one moment, one is at the pinnacle, the next on a slippery slope to losing it all. However, there are usually choices, a series of choices, that lead to that slope. "There is no such thing as a minor lapse of integrity," according to Tom Peters (author of *In Search of Excellence*).

The song "Slow Fade" by Casting Crowns describes it perfectly:

> *Be careful, little eyes, what you see*
> *It's the second glance that ties your hands as*
> *   darkness pulls the strings*
> *Be careful, little feet, where you go*
> *For it's the little feet behind you that are sure*
> *   to follow*
> *It's a slow fade when you give yourself away*
> *It's a slow fade when black and white have*
> *   turned to gray*
> *Thoughts invade, choices are made, a price*
> *   will be paid*
> *When you give yourself away*

People never crumble in a day
It's a slow fade, it's a slow fade
Be careful, little ears, what you hear
When flattery leads to compromise, the end is
*   always near*
Be careful, little lips, what you say
For empty words and promises lead broken
*   hearts astray*
It's a slow fade when you give yourself away
It's a slow fade when black and white have
*   turned to gray*
Thoughts invade, choices are made, a price
*   will be paid*
When you give yourself away
People never crumble in a day
The journey from your mind to your hands
Is shorter than you're thinking
Be careful if you think you stand
You just might be sinking
It's a slow fade when you give yourself away
It's a slow fade when black and white have
*   turned to gray*
Thoughts invade, choices are made, a price
*   will be paid*
When you give yourself away
People never crumble in a day
Daddies never crumble in a day

Families never crumble in a day
Oh be careful, little eyes, what you see
Oh be careful, little eyes, what you see
For the Father up above is looking down
    in love
Oh be careful, little eyes, what you see[1]

Our country is spiraling out of control, as our moral compass is no longer facing true north. I once saw a billboard in Dallas (which is now on TV) advertising a hotel in Las Vegas that read, *just the right amount of wrong.* Is that where we are today in America?

Abraham Lincoln said, "Nearly all men can stand adversity, but if you want to test a man's character, give him power." If you look at the landscape today across the nation, you can see this repeatedly: many people in a power position abuse it to the detriment of the organization and often themselves. Leadership is more about being than doing. Of course, there are skills needed to lead, but ultimately, the character of the leader will always emerge. Honesty is usually at the top of the traits desired when followers are asked what they want in a leader.

Have you noticed that it seems there are no absolutes anymore? I have often heard the phrase, "What's right for you is not right for me." Oh my! Students are finding more ways to cheat. Parents increasingly are supporting students when they violate our rules. (I purposely did not use "break our rules" because the rule is still there. They simply violated what the rule set out to avoid.) When I was growing up, if a teacher called my parents (much less a principal), whatever punishment I got at school would be worse when I got home! Now, sometimes, the parent will come to our campus and challenge the teacher or administrator.

America is losing its moral boundaries. If you read the news, almost daily, leaders are making terrible choices, professionally as well as personally. In almost every profession, there are examples of moral failure. I do not think there is anyone immune from this downfall of moral decline. However, I have witnessed that people have recovered. Many times, though, they had lost so much before they had a chance to redeem themselves.

I have personally experienced seeing how personal choices outside of his profession can ruin a leader's integrity. One's personal life cannot be separated from their professional one. People think initially that they can handle their job, even if they have committed some kind of moral failure. If they do not turn around their actions, soon, their choices and decisions at work will suffer.

With this decline in morality, integrity is at a premium. Living a life of integrity takes conscious decisions and choices every day. J. J. Watt of the N.F.L. Houston Texans says, "Suc-

cess isn't owned, it's leased. And rent is due every day!"
Replace "success" with "integrity," and that is the way a
leader should approach each moment of every day. That is
not just on the job, but it is 24/7. You see, leaders do not have
the luxury of "clocking out." If you have been a leader for any
length of time, you understand that the title of leader follows
you wherever you go.

In education alone, according to a 2007 Associated Press
study conducted between 2001 and 2005, there were 2,570
educators whose teaching credentials were revoked, denied,
surrendered, or sanctioned following allegations of sexual
misconduct. As evidenced in the many headlines regarding
corporate greed, self-serving political leaders, violence, and
school shootings, you can observe that the foundations upon
which our country was built are eroding. As leaders, we need
to model what integrity looks like. We should strive to be the
remnant of what is good, positive, clean, and honorable so
that our followers can gain and keep their trust for us.

I participated in an education law conference a few years ago,
and the following statistics were shared regarding the number
of investigations conducted in Texas in the school year
2014–2015:

- Inappropriate relationships: 188
- Sexual misconduct: 121
- Physical abuse: 189

- Drugs/alcohol: 191

Without trust, we cannot influence. Later in this book, I will devote an entire chapter on trust. If someone asked me to define *leadership* in one word, it would be "influence." I think that is the bottom line for leaders. If we cannot influence our crew, we have no impact. It all begins with *integrity*.

I think there is no better question to ask ourselves than, "Would I follow me?" Whatever the answer, there should be a follow-up question, "Why or why not?"

As leaders, we make moral decisions frequently, especially when it comes to our students' behavior. Virtually every decision we make dealing with discipline is one of morality. Ethical and spiritual issues have always been in school. Schools are, after all, moral institutions. As a result, we should be grounded in morality and integrity. Influence is what leaders do. I have a formula of what leadership is, and influence is half of that formula. However, if you cannot lead with integrity, then you cannot influence.

When it comes to integrity, there is probably no better example than Paul. I am going to refer to a different book and quote of what Paul said in his first letter to the Corinthian church. 1 Corinthians 4:16, Paul says: "Therefore, I exhort you, be imitators of me." When someone says to *be imitators of me*, he must feel confident that he lives a life of integrity.

Now, this was a guy who, whenever he wrote a letter, it became a book of the Bible! That might be a stretch, but the message is that Paul was a great example of what it took to live morally upright.

In the voyage to Rome, he exhibited integrity throughout as he continually gained more trust among the Roman officials. To begin, Paul was able to take two very close friends with him. One was Luke, and the other was Aristarchus. This is unprecedented. It is unclear why or how he was able to have these two accompany him, but I choose to think that the Roman centurion saw Paul as someone he could trust. As to the centurion, each time one is mentioned, you find them to be men of integrity. So we have at least two men of integrity here on this voyage. Paul lived his whole life fearlessly. He lived this way because he knew that the worst thing that could happen to him was to die for Christ, which for him was gain. We continue to learn a great deal from Paul. He lived a life of adversity but was filled with trust, as his Lord was leading him. Being a *wave-maker* is living life and leading fearlessly. The absence of fear is the presence of God. So feel confident as you lead fearlessly, as God will be with you throughout.

As we finish this seventh chapter on our *Wave-Making* voyage, we cannot sail without integrity. Integrity should be a capstone attribute of a leader. Integrity never happens by accident. Integrity happens on purpose. This piece of payload is quite heavy since it involves our choices every day. However, it is nothing that you cannot handle. Let's continue to make a positive difference in kids' lives.

MAKING WAVES

"Integrity is one thing you cannot afford to lose. You can give it away or sell it, but you can't buy it. Without integrity, you become nothing and have nothing."—Michael Josephson

Being a leader first requires personal responsibility, the responsibility to those around you. Remember, there is no such thing as a minor lapse of integrity. You develop integrity over time by choosing to do the right thing *all the time*. Just like trust, integrity is only rented, you never own it.

---

1. Writer: Hohn Mark Hall, Casting Crowns, 2008 used by permission

8

AUTHORITY: THE BUCK STOPS ON YOUR DESK

If you wish to know what a man is, place him in authority.—Proverb

Nearly all men can stand adversity, but if you want to test a man's character, give him power. —Abraham Lincoln

Advice for staff meetings from neuroscience: the brain does not pay attention to boring! Duh!!!

Walk your talk.

Do what is right, not what is easy.

The brain is always at the party, and Leadership

always dances to the tune of the brain.—Mindful Leadership

True leadership is moral authority, not formal authority. Leadership is a choice, not a position. The choice is to follow universal timeless principles, which will build trust and respect from the entire organization. Those with formal authority alone will lose the trust and respect.—Stephen Covey

To build a strong team, you must see someone else's strength as a complement to your weakness and not a threat to your position or authority.—Christine Caine

You are under authority wherever you are. While you drive to work each day, you are under the city or county's authority. Obviously, when you are at work, you are under someone's authority. If you are a leader in any capacity, you are somebody's authority. Whether you are leading a campus or district, you are over someone else. The military is a great example of using authority and how leaders and followers are to respond in any situation. The military, school districts, and companies all have a chain of command that should be adhered to.

A superintendent was addressing his principals at the beginning of the school year with this message.

What I want you principals to understand is that we are now operating under the Navy command model. Right now, as we do the summer work, the ships are all in port. I am the admiral, and you will follow my orders and protocols. In September, the ships will all go to sea, and as the captains of your ship, you are responsible for a successful voyage. I will not second-guess your decisions on how to take command of your ship, because you are in command, even if I am visiting you. But be successful, because the oldest rule of the navy is this: 'If the mission isn't successful, the captain goes down with his ship.'

Sometimes you just have to go first. In my last year as superintendent, my mission was to use technology in the most effective way to enhance my faculty's teaching. We had given each teacher a new iPad the previous year, provided PD on the best ways to use them as a resource. I even had "appy hour," where teachers demonstrated their favorite apps and how they used them in their subject/class. I tried to encourage them to use Twitter and blog. I gave them examples of my Twitter experience and emailed each of them on how to set up their own Twitter page. One of the most fearful risks I did was begin my own blog page. I asked some Twitter friends how to blog and then began. I thought if I was asking my teachers to take risks, I must lead out or go first to set the example.

One definition of authority is the freedom to decide or the right to act without hindrance. Wouldn't it be nice if that last part was true? However, those hindrances might just be part of the system of checks and balances. Those are probably not written in policy, but in practice, they are always there. You are the chief decision-maker. You are looked upon as the one who makes the final decision. Anytime you make a tough call or decision, remember that is only half the job. Living with it is the other half. Some find it easy to make decisions. It is living with consequences that they find difficult. With that much power, take time, collaborate (if possible), and make the best decision possible for what is right for kids. The buck stops at your desk.

I have used a couple of illustrations when I speak on authority. One is the umbrella, and the other is of a bird perched on a limb with two of his young under his wings. I talk about both protecting the one(s) under the umbrella or wings. However, I also point out that when they step out from under that protection, they are now on their own. They lose protection. It is the leader's responsibility to cover or protect.

When the word *authority* is heard, it is often used with power. If you are a leader for any length of time, you have found that power is not unlimited. One thing to keep in mind is that when you use power, you lose power. Roger Goodell, commissioner of the NFL, has seen his power diminish over the last year because he used it in several cases involving players making poor choices. In almost every case, his decision was altered or reduced. You may not lose the power that comes with the position, but you lose the power of influence with your followers. As I have said before, leadership is influence, so use your power very carefully.

There are times when given tough circumstances that you will have to make a hard decision. I have also learned that we often have time to make those decisions. I once heard the phrase that I want to apply here, "paralysis by analysis," meaning that we can sometimes try to consider too many issues, sides, or factors rather than just make what we know is the right call. We all have an inner standard that we live by, so use that standard and apply it to the situation. Make the call.

One of the common phrases I see on police cars is "serve and protect." I will talk about the "serve" part in a later chapter. If you could explain what authority is down to its lowest common denominator, that would define it. When you begin to think about laws, policy, employee handbooks, student handbooks, or codes of conduct, they are there to protect the employees, students, the organization, and the leader. After many years of editing and tweaking handbooks, I like to say that these can be your best friend or worst enemy, depending on what is written. Most handbooks have some kind of template that is usually written by attorneys and are updated each year, depending on what cases are litigated and what the state legislature has changed or new laws added. Those handbooks are truly living documents. You should be very careful in the way you edit your handbook. This should be a collaboration of your inner circle, cabinet, or leadership crew. Do not try to take on this very important task by yourself. However, make sure that you thoroughly vet the final version and make sure you can live with it.

Handbooks, policy, and rules are just created for employees to work within boundaries. The brain likes to know confines in which to work to be productive. The executive function of the brain works at its highest efficiency when it knows (1) what it is working on, (2) that outside destructive influencers are controlled or kept away, and (3) that it is working from relevant information. When all three of these are supplied, the brain has almost unlimited potential. The brain's GPS will work freely to the vision of the leader. Your people will soar.

Just as under all authority, we are all accountable in some way. All of our actions and decisions are accountable. We are free to make any choice, but the consequences are completely out of our control. Teachers are accountable for their students' learning. I often ask, if students do not learn, is teaching occurring? Principals are accountable to the superintendent. The superintendent/CEO is accountable to their board. We are all accountable to our students for their learning and to their parents to enhance the lives of the students under our care.

One thing I tried to never do is blame someone else for the results of my campus or district. I tried never to make excuses. There were many times in my last position that when others made questionable decisions, but the results were my responsibility. That is what makes leadership so difficult. Companies, school districts, campuses, and teams all rise and fall, depending on their leadership. I took the responsibility that the buck truly stopped on my desk.

As I stated in the first sentence of the first chapter, leadership is hard. That is why you get the big bucks. Right? Yes, the buck stops on your desk. You are constantly making decisions, which is quite exhausting. You are persistently tweaking or correcting practices and decisions that your followers make. However, you chose to be a leader so that you could make a difference, and you wanted to transform a campus, district, or organization.

At the beginning of each year, I always stressed to my administrative crew the importance of notifying me if a decision they made could be questioned or controversial. I do not like to use the word *hate*, but I hated being blindsided by parents or board members when I knew nothing about the situation. It is embarrassing, and, worst of all, I had to scramble to answer a question or find a solution that I was not prepared to handle.

The concept of leadership must begin with what I like to call "the lowest common denominator." It encompasses *covering, duty, protection, equipping,* and *direction.* In my presentations, I show a meme of a lion with scratches all over his face with the words, "Everyone wants to be a beast—until it's time to do what real beasts do." (I saw this illustration on Twitter; however, I do not know who originated it.)

There are a plethora of second-guessers, Monday-morning quarterbacks, and backseat drivers. You have to be "the beast" almost every day in your leadership position. Sometimes, someone needs to hear you roar! Before you feel the need to roar, however, you need to be certain that there are no gaps in your alignment with policy, rules, and vision that you have in place. If that is the case, then let it roar!

As I was thinking more about being a beast, of course, you must use your "roar" with great discretion. In *Kingdom Man* by Tony Evans, the author uses lions in the following illustration. Lions in the wild roar for a few reasons. The lion has no natural predator, which is why they are king of the jungle. They roar (1) to protect and scare away intruders, (2) to startle their prey before attacking to act as a provider, (3) to call their scattered pride back home in serving as a leader, and finally, (4) to build relationships. A leader should exercise all of those attributes—protect, provide, partner, and of course, lead. We have the authority to influence and impact our dominion. The bottom line, the lion roars to declare dominion. You should not have to do this often but never back down when it is time to be "the beast" and declare and express your dominion.

In one part of *Kingdom Man*, Tony explains that when there is a problem, an issue, or a concern, he holds up three fingers. Those three fingers stand for three words: "I've got this!" Those three words mean to his family or church that there is no need to worry, to carry the burden, or try to figure it out. "Let me take this, and I will figure what is best." Maybe you could adopt a similar practice for your followers so that they know you have it under control, telling them, "I've got this!"

As Peter Drucker ("founder of modern management" and author of *Concept of Corporation*) says, "Every decision is like surgery. It is an intervention into the system and therefore carries the risk of shock." All big decisions cause a ripple in your crew. Nobody likes to look people in the eye and say "no" or give a negative response to a request. It is very difficult to implement change, but you transform your dominion because that is what is best.

The brain cannot operate efficiently if it is stressed. It actually secretes a stress chemical called cortisol. When you are stressed, cortisol inhibits thinking and learning. Obviously, if people are stressed, their performance drops dramatically. So as one in authority, it is your job to protect your crew so that they can produce exemplary work and remove, not add to, their stress levels, whenever possible.

One piece of advice I gave my inner circle was trying to find a way to say "yes." Then as a last resort, if you must say "no," stand by that decision. Sometimes that is the hard part, standing by your decision. That is why you take the time, study the issue, look at all the possibilities, and go with your decision. Good experience comes in handy in these situations.

Depending on the size of your campus or district, make sure

you are not the only one making decisions. Take advantage of your assistants and delegate some of the decisions to them. Remember, if you can, to include your inner circle to help make big decisions. There will be times that only you can decide. Usually, one thing is usually on your side—time. You typically do not have to make an immediate decision. Think, analyze, collaborate (if possible), and even sleep on it. You will find that this practice will help you make good, sound decisions. Remember, part of your job is making leaders, so take that part of your job seriously. Obviously, there are times when you are the only one to finally decide. That is the reason you were chosen to lead.

One of the worst parts of your job is telling someone they will no longer work for your organization, campus, or district. No matter what they had done to deserve it, looking into their eyes and asking them for their resignation, terminating their employment, or reassigning to another position was the practice I detested the most. I tried to put myself in their shoes and make the experience as easy as I could. I would never use small talk, as I would try to make it as short and direct as possible. This conversation is surely not the first with the employee; I had my documentation, and this would be the final meeting I would have with them. One thing I learned after many years is that this kind of meeting is hardly ever as bad as I thought it would be.

When you begin to realize that you are responsible for

budget, curriculum, personnel (the most time-consuming), custodial and maintenance, students, parents—and I could go on for a while—you realize you are worth every penny you are paid. I know you are probably thinking, *I am worth a whole lot more* (and you probably are), but you are not going to get rich in education. Education is the best profession in the world. We touch the future. Our payback is when a change-maker comes back and tells you that you made a difference in their lives.

In the last week of my job, I was sitting at my desk, and a student named Miranda came and stood in my doorway, her head leaning on the door. In a very sad voice, she said, "Well, you are leaving us." I replied that I was, and teared up. She continued, "I want to ask a favor from you. Would you come back and hand me my diploma when I graduate?" As I type these words, I get choked up again. You see, these are the times when you realize, *this* is why I decided to become a teacher.

All people want structure, boundaries, consistency, and routines, whether they want to admit it or not. It is the job of the leader to make those happen. As I am listing these responsibilities, I realize how big a job you have. It is literally never-ending. I know I have mentioned this before, but if you are the leader, you are always "on." All of you now have cell phones. I remember a time when I went out of town to a conference, and if someone were to call and ask for me, my secretary would respond, "Mr. Roberts is out of town and will be back on... Can I leave a message for him?" Now everyone has your cell number (especially your secretary) and can call with a concern and reach you immediately wherever you are. You can never really get away from it all.

I once attended a seminar sponsored by the Houston Texans. I will never forget what the general manager, Rick Smith, said regarding the media, "We do not talk *to* the media. We talk *through* the media." If you remember that advice, it will serve you well. Develop a positive relationship with the newspaper reporter covering your organization, as well as any other media person you can. If you constantly welcome their calls and visits and call them when something is going to really make your organization shine, then when something negative happens (and it will, given time), you can usually expect to not look too bad when the report is aired or published.

As you know, you can be interviewed for 10–15 minutes and have a dozen questions and answers, but the segment will last about 45 seconds on TV or one or two quotes from you in the newspaper. Never try to "spin" the story. Always tell the truth and never say, "No comment." Simply say, "Let me get back to you on that when I have all the information that you need so that your report will be accurate." I like to add that last part to put a little responsibility on the media to report accurately and truthfully.

As you know, I was an athlete blessed to compete at the highest level. I also coached for almost twenty years. For a long time in education, this seemed to be the path of many educational leaders. After coaching, they would get into administration and see how far they could go up that ladder. I am biased in thinking that athletes and coaches make good leaders because they are naturally competitive. They want to win. I started competing when I was in the fourth grade. I hate to lose, no matter what the game. Athletes also have one advantage over those who have not competed in the arena. They know how to respond to adversity, whether it is during the game or getting together after a tough loss, or just griping about a demanding coach.

These two attributes, desire to win and response to adversity, are necessary to be an effective leader. Can non-athletes become great leaders? Of course, but they must learn those traits over time.

We are in a constant battle. In Paul's letter to the Ephesians, he said, "For our struggle is not against flesh and blood, but against the rulers, against the powers, against the world forces of this darkness, against the spiritual forces of wickedness in the heavenly places" (Eph. 6:12). I think it is important to note here that we are fighting many. Notice in that verse, it lists rulers, powers, and forces. As believers, we are not just fighting against Satan, but his army, as well. Satan can only be in one place at one time.

We are in a constant battle against an enemy that is invisible but very real. The enemy knows us maybe better than we know ourselves. That enemy even has authority over an army. Another advantage of coaches is that they know how to plan against an opponent. Coaches spend countless hours studying the opponent and their plan and tendencies, just like a general of troops studies his enemy. Paul often referenced athletes, athletic contests, and battles.

In Acts 27: 21, we read, "Then Paul stood up in their midst." This was when Paul began to be *the* authority on the ship. This was when the storm was raging, and all the men on the ship were scared and were looking for someone to take charge. I want to stress that Paul did not supplant anyone's authority. However, he did know the Supreme Authority, and through that authority, Paul was able to step forward. It seemed like Paul was the only one on the ship who knew what to do. The Roman captain was not leading, the Roman pilot did not know how to steer, so he was not steering at all, and the centurion was frightened. As a result, Paul was the authority who took command.

Paul was constantly under authority from the ultimate ruler and the ultimate king, so he was always protected. He could act in complete freedom and without fear. He knew he could always be a fearless leader.

It is often during times of crisis that true leaders emerge. I pray that you never have to experience any crisis. But if you do, you need to bear the burdens, find the solutions, and win the victories when everyone else is merely flustered, confounded, and perplexed.

As we continue to load our ship on this leadership voyage, we have to include authority. There is quite a lot to pack with this load, as it carries more weight than most other necessities that we packed. However, we chose this job, now we must make the most of it. Let's see how serving as a leader with authority can enhance our students' lives. Make Waves!

MAKING WAVES

As a leader, you are given authority. Harry Truman maybe said it best, "It is understanding that gives us an ability to have peace. When we understand the other fellow's viewpoint and he understands ours, then we can sit down and work out our differences. The buck stops here."

As the authority you are, the *compass* for *direction, coun-*

sel/judge for wise *decisions* and the *benchmark/standard* for *evaluation*.

In my presentations, I show a picture of a donkey walking across a clothesline by the artist Robert Deybar....getting that image in your head? I just say seven words: "Your ass is always on the line."

9

CHANGE IS HARD

Change is inevitable; growth is optional.

Don't fear failure. Fear being in the exact same place next year as you are today.—Michael Hyatt

Change is messy! So provide a long runway.

Transformation literally means going beyond your form.—Wayne Dyer

Change requires courage, commitment, and effort.

One thing you can always count on in education is change.

You were not hired to keep the status quo. From my experiences, every time I was hired, it was to make an improvement, to change the culture, or (for my last job) to create a school. The late legendary basketball coach, John Wooden, said, "make every day a masterpiece." If you begin your day with that mindset, think what results you could achieve! The leader creates the culture of every organization. You were hired to change or improve—as my friend and Twitter PLN member, Jimmy Casas (@jimmycasas), signs off, "be the change" and never be satisfied with keeping the status quo.

Change is all about transformation. The brain continually looks for patterns. As a result, when change takes place, the brain has to adjust to something that breaks a pattern and searches for something familiar. The brain looks to the merits and potential of what might be familiar and comfortable. It has a bias to things that are ingrained, so anytime you attempt to transform, begin with something familiar and build from there. I like to say, "begin by creating a long runway and let them build momentum."

In my first principal job, I coined the phrase, "side by side, we enhance the lives of the students we teach," as a theme to work from. This came from two very different sources. I had the pleasure of working a church youth camp where I was blessed to chauffeur a teenage singer from Australia named Rebecca St. James from the airport to our campsite. Rebecca was on her way to becoming a star in Christian music.

In the couple of days of driving her to our camp from her hotel, I learned a little about her, and her heart for advancing the kingdom through her music. One song she sang at her concert was "Side by Side," which had a big impact on me. When I heard her sing the lyrics, I immediately thought that is the way a school should run. The message is that we walk this journey together—every day, every valley, we walk, side by side. You can depend on me, arm in arm, hand in hand, side by side.

The second half of the phrase came from gifted author and motivational speaker, Harry Wong. When I heard him speak, he suggested that every educator should have business cards. He said that under our name should be the words, "Professional Educator." He also suggested that if someone asks, "what do you do?" to reply, "I am a professional educator, and I enhance the lives of the students I teach." As a result, I put those two phrases together. Those words could work for any school leader, or any leader. In any other organization, one could substitute *customer* for "student." I wanted my teachers to not only teach content and curriculum, but to—maybe more importantly—enhance our students' lives.

I tried to work from a theme each year. One time, my theme

was completely by accident. My first year as high school principal, my superintendent came to me and said, "we need to leave in about fifteen minutes to attend a district meeting." I immediately thought, *I have about ten minutes in my first faculty meeting to make some kind of impact.* My mind began to race as to what I could say in that length of time that would make any kind of difference. I remembered I had just finished reading *Standing Tall* by Steve Farrar. There was a chapter called "Ridin' for the Brand" in it that I thought would fit. Steve Farrar got this idea from the book of the same title written by Louis L'Amour.

That summer, 33 new teachers, three new counselors, three new assistant principals, and a new band director were hired. As a result, about a third of our faculty was new. So with the beginning of the chapter, "Ridin' for the Brand," this is what I shared with my faculty and staff that morning:

The Brand. Every man and boy in the Old West knew the importance of a brand. A brand was the mark that a rancher would burn on his stock. But it was more than that; much more. When a man hooked up with a certain outfit, it was then said he was "ridin' for the brand."

The term "riding for the brand" was an expression of loyalty to a man's employer or the particular outfit he rode for. It was considered a compliment of the highest order in an almost feudal society. If a man did not like the ranch or the way they conducted their affairs, he was free to quit, and many did, but if he stayed on, he gave loyalty and expected it.

A man was rarely judged by his past, only his actions. Many a man who came West left things behind him he would rather forget, so it was not the custom to ask questions. Much was forgiven if a man had courage and integrity and if he did his job. If a man gave less than his best, somebody had to take up the slack, and he was not admired.

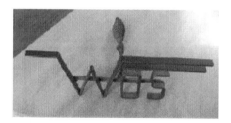

When I finished reading, my head football coach came to me and said he loved this and that he was going to use it some way with his football team. The drill team director made t-shirts for a fundraiser with the summary quoted on the back. The announcer for football used it every game in the introductions. The welding teacher even made me a brand. I still have that brand!

The best confirmation happened a couple of months into the year. I overheard a couple of men (a teacher and an assistant principal) raising their voices. They kept on arguing—I did not want it to get out of hand, so I walked out of my office... and then *it happened!* One of them said, "you are just not ridin' for the brand!" They had bought into what I wanted and internalized it. I realized then that a theme was not to be taken lightly. Later in my career, I would order custom lapel pins that I would give to every staff member: custodians, cafeteria workers, bus drivers, teachers, and administrators. They would either put them on their lanyards or name badges and wore them all year. Some never took the old one off and had several on their lanyards. Some even anticipated and wondered, "What is going to be the theme this year?" before I would reveal it at the initial faculty meeting.

"Navigate the rapids" was used when Texas changed the entire testing and accountability system. I used "add a li'l chocolate" when I wanted to stress building positive relationships. The third pin illustrated when Dave Burgess presented his *Teach Like a Pirate* message to open our professional development, and that became our theme.

I tried to use these pins to help with creating culture in our school. One of the best examples of creating a positive culture is Walt Disney World. If you ask a Disney employee, *any* employee, what their product is, the reply will be, "we create happiness." Wouldn't that be a great reply for a classroom, campus, or district?

On one of my slides in my presentation, I show this picture of a Disney security officer handing a pen and notepad to a very young girl dressed as Cinderella. He makes a practice anytime he sees a little girl similarly dressed to ask, "Excuse me, princess, can I have your autograph?" If that were your daughter, how would you feel? How do you think the young girl felt after? Doesn't it put a smile on your face?

If you are going to be successful in your campus or district, remember this: newer rules, procedures, programs, or technology are not the answer; nor is a cleverly worded theme for the year. Themes can come off as very hollow-sounding when the leader is not sincere. On the other hand, transforming your school with contagious practices will empower your employees to make a difference.

The last year of my superintendency, I transformed my faculty meetings. I got the idea on Twitter as I participated in the many chats available and noticed how much teachers did not like faculty meetings. As a result, I wanted to only conduct faculty meetings that had nothing to do with management. If I could cover it in an email, I would not cover it in a faculty meeting. I wanted it to be about curriculum, pedagogy, or technology. For example I flipped a meeting (assigned a TED Talk then discussed at the next meeting), held a QR-code scavenger hunt, Skyped with a world-class author/presenter (Julie Adams), did a book study, enjoyed an "Appy Hour" (where teachers presented their favorite app), had fun with augmented reality, and showed how to backchannel with TodaysMeet (now defunct).

When you took the job you are presently in, you changed the culture almost immediately because you came in—not necessarily for better or worse, just different. When you moved into your office, you hung different pictures, maybe moved the desk, placed your diplomas on the wall, and probably made many other changes because you wanted that office to be yours. You put your "brand" on your office. You should take a few minutes of your day and notice what your campus culture is by just perusing what you see on the walls, in the hallways, cafeteria, and your office area. What is the message you are sending? Is it positive, welcoming, or is it about rules and consequences?

A verse in Paul's second letter to the Corinthian church is what I think of when I hear the word *transformation*. Second Corinthians 5:17 says, "Therefore, if anyone is in Christ, he is a new creation. The old has passed away; behold, the new has come." This means that when a person asks the Lord to come into his life, he is transformed, a completely new person. That is one of the greatest promises in scripture.

Also, examining our current scripture, in Acts 27, remember that Paul began this journey as a prisoner. In the end, he was transformed into the leader of the ship. Paul's position did not happen overnight, and neither will anything you try to change. Lead change with confidence, good planning, and collaboration, and your transformation will be a positive one.

Paul's story and the verse above show the power of God when He decides to demonstrate it. What an awesome God we have and serve!

As we continue to pack our bags for our leadership voyage, we are certain to put transformation in our luggage. Transformation might be the toughest to attain since it requires

change. However, that is why we are in leadership, to facili-
tate change or transformation. Make Waves!

MAKING WAVES

It's not about perfect. It's about effort. And when you bring
that effort every single day, that's where transformation
happens. That's how change occurs.

One child, one teacher, one book, one pen can change the
world.—Malala Yousafzai

Transformation is not five minutes from now; it's a present
activity. At this moment, you can make a different choice, and
it's these small choices and successes that build up over time
to help cultivate a healthy self-image and self-esteem.

10

TRUST IS NEVER OWNED — IT'S ONLY RENTED

You cultivate trust by building relationships, setting a clear direction, giving people what they need to see it through, and getting out of their way.

Leadership is about loving and empowering the people who trust and embrace your vision for the future.

Trust takes time to build, seconds to break, and forever to repair.

Trusting you is my decision. Proving me right is your choice.

Trust is the cornerstone of leadership. Without gaining and inspiring trust from your followers, you will never be able to lead effectively. If you do not have trust, you will never be able to influence. If you cannot influence, you are not leading. Leadership can be defined by one word: *influence*. Some leaders lead organizations without trust and merely "lead with an iron fist" with a "my way or the highway" kind of leadership. However, they may not last or might have a tremendously difficult time getting results they desire. Do not get me wrong; it is not always sunshine and rainbows with leaders who are trusted. At times, they must be firm and make tough decisions that are not popular. But, in the end, because they built positive, healthy relationships, their followers knew it was what was best for the organization.

That is why integrity is so important in leading people. I once had a parent share with me words that I count as my biggest compliment. He said, "Hal, you walk your talk." After that conversation, I felt like I had made a difference. One head coach in my school called another head coach from my former school as high school principal and asked about me. The latter stated, "He will do what he says he will do."

In the book *The Thin Book of Trust,* Charles Feltman defines trust this way, "choosing to risk making something you value vulnerable to another person's actions." When he thinks of distrust, it is, "deciding that what is important to me is not safe with this person in this situation (or any situation)." This is a pretty big deal in leadership because if there's no trust, there's no connection.

When you think about culture in any organization, trust *must* be a foundation! If trust is not part of your culture, you will not like the culture that is present. You always have a culture —just make sure it is a culture that is advancing your core values.

I am sure you have noticed at this point in this voyage of leadership that you cannot lead without people. You cannot get results that you strive for without assistance from others. As you are working with people, your words will carry more weight than you could imagine. When you gain trust from people, they are more open with you. You begin to get constructive comments. People come to you more freely to give good suggestions. With trust, the relationships that I spoke about earlier will be easier, more positive, and helpful. Your job becomes easier. I will never say that a leader's job is easy, but gaining trust will make it more manageable.

Even though athletics was a huge part of my life and had a great impact with me, I think *teamwork* is overused and does not carry the weight that maybe it should. The district that I served as superintendent used *family* instead of teamwork. When I arrived, it was a pre-K–8 district with approximately 350 students and had its centennial celebration the year before. I remember the board used *family* a few times during the two interviews that I had. I recalled one question that was asked: "What will you do to keep the family atmosphere as we begin to grow and add a high school?" I responded that even in large families, you just give more love as each child arrives. There is more love to share. I remember before the birth of my second child that I was scared that I would not love her like I did the first. However, God gives us that much more love to share when more children are born.

Both *team* and *family* are good descriptions of a healthy organization, one in which the culture is positive and collaborative. Whatever term you use, make sure that you understand it, live by it, and are vigilant to make it smooth-running.

As I have been writing this book, I have been texting with a parent on Friday nights to check on the football team from my last school. She gives me status reports throughout the game. At the end of one game, I told her, "thank you for doing this for me." She responded, "thank you for loving our kids." In education, if you love the kids in your class/campus/district, it will always return in dividends and, usually earn the trust of your parents. As I have never worked in the corporate world, I do not know for certain how everything works there;

however, James Kouzes and Barry Ponders have studied corporations and businesses for a long time. In their book *Encouraging the Heart: A Leader's Guide to Rewarding and Recognizing Others*, they found only one common characteristic among the most successful CEOs—*affection*. Those CEOs cared for their people, and, in turn, their employees performed better and gained trust in their leader. The best way to gain trust is to love people. As long as the relationships are positive and healthy, this should be your first step in building trust with your crew.

Gaining and keeping trust is not easy. Stephen Covey says, "trust is the glue of life. It's the most essential ingredient in effective communication. It's the foundational principle that holds all relationships." Sometimes it can take a long time to create trust among your followers. However, it can take only moments to lose it. I spoke to this in the integrity chapter, but every decision you make can have an effect on those who trust you, especially when it comes to discipline, support, and those employees who have questionable performance. Unfortunately, in each of these areas, the decision is rarely "black and white," so you are probably not going to please all.

Earlier in this book, I wrote about how all leaders should have an inner circle in the leadership crew. You have to have complete trust in those whom you allow to serve in that circle. You will have tough conversations, make future plans, and make decisions that will affect the whole organization. As those decisions are made and plans implemented, that inner circle must leave personal feelings or opinions in that office or room, and be united when the decisions to move forward have begun. All the questions, feelings, and ideas must be left in that room as you move forward with the decision of the inner circle.

As I type these words using "circle" and "trust," it reminds me of the movie *Meet the Parents*. At one point, Robert DeNiro is explaining the "circle of trust," considering whether his future son-in-law (Ben Stiller) is good enough for his daughter. For those fathers who have daughters, you can absolutely appreciate his conviction, just maybe not to the same extent to which he takes it.

Anytime you step into a new position of leadership, you should immediately begin to build a climate of trust. Build positive relationships, and then trust will follow. If you have noticed throughout this voyage of leadership, it is an everyday endeavor. You must have a purpose every day. However, you can accomplish this—as Nike says, "just do it!" Trust will take you a long way in building your crew to follow you. Trust will give you the gateway to influence.

You may be wondering, *where do I begin with gaining trust??* Start by showing your crew that you care. Get to know them on a level that is outside of their position. Get to know about their family and interests. Meet with them individually just to listen to them. As you see them outside of your office, ask about their kids or hobbies. When people know that you care, they are drawn to you, and you will begin to gain and keep their trust.

Another way to inspire trust is to let your crew know that you failed. I once had a faculty meeting with my last agenda item, "Words from my heart." When I got to that item, I had a long pause and said, "I am not a very good principal." I went on to explain those words and feelings. As a result, one of my harshest critics said in a somewhat loud voice, something to this effect, "This really fires me up, and I appreciate your honesty!" As a result of those words, I gained new and fresh respect and trust from my crew. That was one of the hardest things I have done—to admit that I failed—but in the end, I gained a lot of trust because they saw a vulnerable side to me. I humbled myself before my entire faculty. Humility in a leader will pave the way for trust.

As I was writing this chapter, there was a presidential race for 2016. If you Google "presidential race and trust," you will find millions of hits. The point I am making is that the top candidate in each party scored over 60 percent as being not honest and trustworthy. A 2016 Gallup poll showed 79 percent saying that Congress is out of touch with the average

American, 52 percent saying Congress is corrupt, and 69 percent believing Congress is only focused on special interests. All of this is to say that our country's leadership is in a crisis. If you ask most people, the top priority of a leader should be integrity, honesty, or trustworthiness. We need people in leadership that we can trust.

There are several ways a leader can lose the trust of his crew. One of the worst ways to lose trust is to "spin" the truth. Just always tell the truth; it may hurt initially, but in the long run, you can keep the trust of your crew. Over my thirty years of leadership, I learned the value of availability. The old cliché, "my door is always open," should be adhered to. In the chapter on immersion, I showed that being among your crew is very important. If someone asks you to keep something confidential, you better keep that promise. You will lose that trust very quickly if you happen to share something that was said in confidence with someone else. I often told others, "I may have to share this with someone," if I saw it was something I might have to talk about later. If you fall short on commitments, that is a surefire way to lose trust. Delivering more than you promise is the best way to keep that trust.

As you know by now, Paul rose to obtain a leadership role on his voyage to Rome. You might have figured that Paul had to gain much trust before he could take over a ship that was under the authority of Roman soldiers. He must have gained that trust through many actions, words, and decisions, and by continuing to fulfill every prediction and every promise he gave. Over many weeks, Paul continually walked his talk. If you go back to the book of Acts, you will find that Paul even gained the trust of the centurion who was guarding him. Once Paul was converted, he was "all in" on his witness and was arguably the best disciple and soul-winner for Christ.

As leaders, we must constantly be aware of our actions and words. Sometimes, one single choice can destroy the trust that you have worked so hard to achieve. We must walk our talk. Our goal should be to deliver more than we promise. Let's continue to load our ship for our leadership voyage, including trust. Trust is an everyday item, so it will be quite heavy— maybe even a burden, but that burden is very valuable. So when we carry trust on this brigantine, we should guard carefully. Trust will carry us far as we serve our students and crew. Make Waves!

MAKING WAVES

The captain of a ship had absolute authority when fighting or pursuing another ship. However, the quartermaster was the "trustee" of the ship. He would often lead the crew when attacking another vessel. He was like a judge and would settle disputes and had the authority to punish with whipping or drubbing. These men were elected, just as the captain was. So the crew looked to the performance of these two leaders. They could be removed at any time from the crew with a majority vote. So the leaders had to gain trust to continue to lead. It was not with words but by actions that the crew gained trust from their leaders.

11

THERE IS MAGIC IN ENTHUSIASM & EXCITEMENT

Knowledge is power, but enthusiasm pulls the switch.—Ivan Bull

There is real magic in enthusiasm. It spells the difference between mediocrity and accomplishment.—Norman Vincent Peale

Enthusiasm is excitement with inspiration, motivation, and a pinch of creativity.—Bo Bennett

Live the truth. Express your love. Share your enthusiasm. Take action towards your dreams. Walk your talk. Dance and sing to your music.

Embrace your blessings. Make today worth remembering.—Dr. Steve Maraboli

Ralph Waldo Emerson said, "enthusiasm is the mother of effort, and without it, nothing great was ever achieved." The first part of that quote is rarely mentioned, but it is important to note. Enthusiasm begins with effort. You will never see a lazy person referred to as enthusiastic.

Passion and enthusiasm go together; however, there is one big difference. You can fake enthusiasm, but not passion. The phrase "fake it 'til you make it," applies to enthusiasm. Even on down days, you can fake enthusiasm. I tried never to show that I was down when I was around students. I believe I owed them my best at all times. As I reflect on my leadership, neither could I ever fake or cover my emotions with my secretaries. They could always tell when something was wrong.

One area that seems to always motivate me is my Professional Learning Network on Twitter. I cannot tell you how important it is to get connected. You can ask questions, express concerns, get ideas, and, for almost any other area where you need help, you can glean assistance from your PLN. I will say one thing, and I believe others will agree: if you need help, your PLN is there for you. If you have not yet connected on Twitter, do that now—not tomorrow, not next week, but *now*. You will not regret it, and will be amazed at the support and how much influence you will have when you begin to participate in Twitter chats. Every time I have made a presentation, I have had educators tell me that they follow me on Twitter and that I have inspired them in some way. I am not sharing that to tell you how inspirational I am, but to plead with you to experience what I have been fortunate to see. I have been able to make real friends as a result. When I have cited my friends on Twitter, I have included their handle. Follow all of them! You will learn from some of the best and brightest professional educators in the country. The educators on Twitter are progressive with fresh ideas, and they will inspire you to be better. They can make you enthusiastic about your job.

When I looked up the root word for *enthusiasm*, I found that it originated in Latin from Greek *enthousiasmos*, from *enthous*, "possessed by a god, inspired" (based on *theos*, or *god*). When a leader is enthusiastic about their job, it is contagious just like passion is. Imagine what a culture could be if all your staff were enthusiastic about their jobs.

The brain does not pay attention to boring things. We learn better if we are engaged. Likewise, our crew will perform better if they are engaged. Of course, it is not your job to always try to inspire the people in your organization. True professionals should not have to be inspired all the time. That should come from within. However, every chance you get to stand before your staff, it is your job to inspire, motivate, and influence them. Sometimes it is not what you say but how you say it. Other times, make sure your words are uplifting. You should also understand that the brain needs breaks. If you have a thirty-minute meeting, there should be some kind of break in the middle. After ten to fifteen minutes, the brain starts to lose attention. Sometimes I would wonder why my faculty would not remember something; after all, it was on the agenda. I talked about it, but then I would realize it was mentioned at about the twenty-minute mark. They lost attention. Adult brains need a break as well.

Being enthusiastic about your job may be hard at times. There are students to manage, teachers to guide, and parents with whom you will meet. However, if you cannot find a way to get enthusiastic most of the time, I would begin to question your love and passion for leading people. As I said in the first chapter, leadership is hard. It is not for everyone. Virtually all of the time, there is one leader for an organization. Does that leader make all the decisions? Probably not. However, it is that leader to whom everyone looks when there are problems to solve, issues to address, communication to be delivered, and a vision to pursue. You are the guy, the man, the woman, the leader that all want to see lead. We probably all pursued leadership to lead more than manage.

As you know all too well, it is management that takes most of your time. I have often seen or heard that managers work in the system and do things right; leaders work on the system and do the right thing. Your job as a leader is to influence to get results.

If your crew always sees you as unenthusiastic, you will find that they will eventually fall away from your leadership. I will have to admit this was one area where I needed work. I had a passion, and I even felt enthusiastic, but there were times that my actions did not show that. You have to consciously show enthusiasm so that it comes across to your whole crew.

I understand that there will be times when you stand before your crew, when addressing problems with enthusiasm is not the most effective way to communicate. I can remember times when I simply sat in a chair and talked about a serious issue with a low volume and tone to make an impact. Changing your delivery method is just as important as showing enthusiasm in getting your point across.

Some of you may be thinking, "Hal, that is just not my personality to act enthusiastic most of the time." Believe me, I understand; however, you need to show enthusiasm some of the time. You want your faculty to show enthusiasm to their students—in fact, I bet you expect it when you observe them in the classroom. Don't you think that you owe it to them to model that at least some of the time?

I asked my friend of over thirty years, Mitzi Neely (@mitzi-neely), what enthusiasm means to her. What she sent me is quite verbose, but that is her, especially when it comes to enthusiasm! I thought I might cut some, but everything she says is so good that I chose to leave it as she wrote. She writes:

Whenever I hear the word *enthusiasm*, I immediately associate it with those individuals who are energetic, passionate, eager, and spirited. Of course, that connection comes from my being one of those people. I believe it is my enthusiasm that prompted the author to ask me to contribute to this book. I first met Hal in 1985 when we became teaching colleagues at an area high school. He was refreshing to work with because of his positive outlook and passion about the profession. We drove people crazy with our response to the question, 'How are you today?' Our answer would always be, 'If it gets any better, I'm not going to be able to stand it.' You can imagine the eye rolls and the deep sighs.

But that's how we felt. We were both enthusiastic and excited about the work we were doing and very blessed to work with kids who offered so much personality, passion, and promise for the future. You see, I love my life. I love my role as an educator, and I love working with kids and teachers. My perspective comes from being a long-time high school teacher, an elementary and high school principal, a curriculum director, and an assistant superintendent.

The passion and enthusiasm for what I do started very early in life. By the age of six, I knew I wanted to be a teacher, and there would be very little to get in the way of achieving that goal. Thirty-five years later, I can tell you I love it more today than when I started.

One of my favorite quotes by Walter Chrysler says, "The real secret of success is enthusiasm." Well, if enthusiasm is what makes the difference, then we all better get some. I believe, to some extent, people come into this life equipped with enthusiasm. We just feel it deep in our bones. Just get me started on a topic I'm excited about, and I can usually get you fired up too.

Effective leaders have a long list of qualities, but passion is a must. Passion breeds enthusiasm. Your colleagues and those that follow you watch what you're doing and the direction you are headed. It's about creating a culture and climate that others believe in. It's about leading where others haven't gone before. It's about making the work meaningful. It's about collaboration, connectedness, and communication.

It's about being a champion for ALL kids. One of my favorite people in the whole world is a deputy superintendent in a nearby district, who has been a champion for kids for 36 years. In fact, I call her a "game-changer." She is deliberate, passionate, formidable, and tireless. She believes in the work they are doing, and those who share in the work share the vision. She leads quietly by example and with more energy and dedication than most people have in their pinky finger. As educators and leaders, part of who we are and what we do is thinking of others before ourselves—always with the sole purpose of creating and nurturing our "this century" thinkers.

We, as leaders, should never assume that quiet and calm equals a lack of passion and strength. We should never mistake kindness for weakness. Because you never know who might be dreaming up the next big thing in their peaceful moments.

It is important to love what you're doing and to empower others to make the journey with you. There has to be someone in leadership to lead the charge. Don't expect to move others if you haven't moved yourself. In Ephesians 6:7, we are commanded to "work with enthusiasm, as though you were working for the Lord rather than for people." What a wonderful reminder for us to serve wholeheartedly and with goodwill. May our actions be contagious and a light of joy to share with others.

My friend and colleague Dave Burgess includes a great quote in his presentations that speaks volumes for the work we do. He said, "light yourself on fire with enthusiasm, and people will come from miles around just to watch you burn!" How true that is. Enthusiasm is so much more than being a cheerleader of sorts. It's about spending time with others and building genuine, authentic relationships. It's about spreading joy. It's about never giving up; never wavering from the goal. It's about never being satisfied with the status quo.

Everything we do has an impact on the students and teachers we work with. The decisions we have to make as leaders are not always easy. Decisions can be painful, challenging, random, and unexpected. Although many times adversity builds barriers, we must continue to stand strong, hold to the course, and push through these barriers. We must "hold the vision, trust the process."

I am more passionate and enthusiastic about the work we are doing in our schools today than ever before. There is so much to be done as we continue to move our change-makers forward. But getting there will take all of us working together. We didn't get where we are by resting on past rewards and accomplishments. What we do takes hard work, commitment, perseverance, energy, enthusiasm, focus, and persistence if we are to move people where they need to be.

In the words of Aldous Huxley, "The secret of genius is to carry the spirit of the child into old age, which means never losing your enthusiasm." I'm counting on that.

I do not know of another person in the Bible who is more enthusiastic or passionate about his ministry, message, or mission than Paul. He never wavered from his mission. Paul was fearless during his Christian life. He was bold in his witness, fearless with his message, and enthusiastic about his walk as a believer.

In his letter to the Philippian church, he said,

For to me, to live is Christ, and to die is gain. But if I am to live on in the flesh, this will mean fruitful labor for me; and I do not know which to choose. But I am hard-pressed from both directions, having the desire to depart and be with Christ, for that is very much better (Phil. 1:21–23).

He is the ultimate example of loyalty and commitment. He also fearlessly lived his life, especially his time on the voyage to Rome. He never wavered through all the obstacles, enemies, shipwrecks, and beatings. Paul was definitely possessed by God, and it showed throughout his life.

As we load the next piece of cargo of enthusiasm, it might be heavy for some and light for others. However, we cannot leave it behind. Before we lift our anchors to sail away, make sure enthusiasm is aboard. Make Waves!

MAKING WAVES!

Enthusiasm is one of the most powerful engines of success. When you do a thing, do it with all your might. Put your whole soul into it. Stamp it with your own personality. Be active, be energetic and faithful, and you will accomplish your object. Nothing great was ever achieved without enthusiasm.—Ralph Waldo Emerson

Enthusiasm is the sparkle in your eyes, the swing in your gait, the grip of your hand, the irresistible surge of will and energy to execute your ideas.—Henry Ford

HUMILITY IS SHOWING VULNERABILITY

Humility is not denying your strength, but accepting your weaknesses.—Rick Warren

Humility is not thinking less of yourself, it is thinking of yourself less. —C.S. Lewis

Humility is the mother of all virtues, courage the father, integrity the child, and wisdom the grandchild.—Stephen R. Covey

God opposes the proud but gives grace to the humble.—James 4:6

Pride is concerned with *who* is right; Humility is concerned with *what* is right.—Ezra T. Benson

I wrestled with (and ultimately decided against) having this chapter in my first book since it did not fit in the PIRATE acronym. I hesitated including it in this book because I felt I could not do it justice. However, God did not let me get it out of my mind. It seemed that an article I would read, a book that I perused, and even a sermon that was preached, humility kept coming up. I do truly believe that humility is a vital attribute for a leader of significance. In Brené Brown's book *Dare to Lead,* she uses the phrase, "you can't get to courage without rumbling with vulnerability...embrace the suck." She means that it takes courage to be vulnerable and allowing yourself to take down your walls or armor to let others see your transparency. She uses over 400,000 pieces of data, including interviews of 150+ C-level leaders, military leaders, and many other sources of data to back up her claims. She discusses vulnerability in great detail and how important it is for a leader to possess—maybe THE most important attribute. I think one cannot be vulnerable without first possessing humbleness.

Exhibiting humility is not in many of our comfort zones. I know in my past positions, I wanted my followers to believe that I knew most of the answers. Because of my 30 years in leadership, I did know a lot, but there was something every year that challenged my knowledge and experience. To many, humility and vulnerability show weakness. I am here to say it shows the opposite—it reveals strength and courage. Courageous leadership requires one to face fear. I used the phrase "lead fearlessly" in my title in my first book and this trait—humility—may be the most important for obtaining fearless leadership. To borrow a line from the movie *Green Book*, "it takes courage to change people's heart." And leading with the heart is the way to significance, not through fear or "my way or the highway" kind of leadership.

The word courage comes from the Latin root *cor*, which means heart (denoting the heart as the seat of feelings or emotions). Leadership requires some courage. Anytime you step in front of others and give them your vision, that takes courage. So, you see, courage is leading from the heart, with the heart. If you think about it, you either lead from your head or lead from your heart. I'm surely not saying to only lead from the heart; just make sure you make it part of your leadership arsenal. The head leads from logic, data, and what could go wrong. The heart leads from humility, vulnerability, and what might make waves or create significance.

Most people are drawn to those that are humble, but have difficulty exhibiting humility to others because they either view their own interests as more important, or are afraid they will be taken advantage of. Humility is risky. There are times when your humble service goes unnoticed, will be unappreciated, or be used for someone else's gain. Humility does not take something from you—it does something for you. Humility or vulnerability is one of the best ways to change the trajectory of your leadership.

There were a few times in past faculty meetings that I said, "I am not a very good principal/superintendent," times when I realized that I had handled a problem in the wrong way and most knew I had. But when I did admit my humbleness and vulnerability, most of my staff rallied around me, lifted me up, grew closer, and became stronger. As a result, I became a little more courageous in my decision-making. Leaders make decisions constantly, and it is by those choices that we are judged.

Leaders may make dozens of choices or decisions in a day. Experiencing fatigue or exhaustion is one of the times that you should never make big decisions. The acronym HALT (Hungry, Angry, Lonely, or Tired) will warn you of emotions you want to avoid when making such decisions. It's a good idea to have HALT posted somewhere you can be reminded of when you are making any kind of decision that will make a big impact.

When you decide to demonstrate humbleness, you sign up to get your butt kicked and for possible failure. But if you never take risks and stay in your comfort zone, you will never experience courage or fearlessness. In that same vein, I do not think you can be innovative or creative. The first time I saw this quote was in our field house at the University of Houston. It made a big impression on me then, and think it is important to share with you.

It is not the critic who counts; not the man who points out how the strong man stumbles, or where the doer of deeds could have done them better. The credit belongs to the man who is actually in the arena, whose face is marred by dust and sweat and blood; who strives valiantly; who errs, who comes short again and again, because there is no effort without error and shortcoming; but who does actually strive to do the deeds; who knows great enthusiasms, the great devotions; who spends himself in a worthy cause; who at the best knows in the end the triumph of high achievement, and who at the worst, if he fails, at least fails while daring greatly, so that his place shall never be with those cold and timid souls who neither know victory nor defeat.—Theodore Roosevelt

---

Right below that was another sign that read,

1. God
2. Country
3. Family

4. UH Cougars

This is a pretty good list of priorities.

I saw a similar quote when I was a high school football player after a tough loss, found on the following week's scouting report:

I am sore, wounded but not slain. I will lay me down and bleed a while and then rise up and fight again. — John Dryden

---

Both of these quotes are for the people who are making those tough calls. It is for those who show up day after day, giving it their best shot. The greatest arenas in leadership are vulnerability, leading from the heart, and staying humble.

Each night when my wife and I turn off the lights, we pray together. One of the things we always pray is for our gratitude or thankfulness for all the moments of our day. They can be)and often are) the small everyday experiences that most would see as insignificant. Some examples are grocery shopping together, cooking together, watching a grandchild perform, and even watching TV together. These simply make each day special and even extraordinary. Maybe you can also do this at the end of your day and journal those special moments that you experience.

Recently in my research, I came across a Japanese phrase; *"wabi-sabi."* We are all imperfect, and this principle is accepting your imperfections and making the most of life. In education or most businesses, nothing is certain. To me, that means anything is possible. I usually focused on what could go wrong, not what is right. As leaders, we are often driven toward perfection, especially in achievements. This drive often leads to stress and anxiety, which we all know is not good for your health, nor the health of your organization.

Breaking down wabi-sabi, *wabi* is defined as "rustic simplicity" or "understated elegance, which really means less is more thinking." *Sabi* is translated to "taking pleasure in the imperfect." Wabi-sabi just invites pause, to focus on blessings (see above) and to celebrate the now and how things are. In Richard Powell's book *Wabi Sabi Simple,* he says it this way, "a way of life that appreciates and accepts complexity while at the same time values simplicity...nothing lasts, nothing is finished, and nothing is perfect." A great example of *wabi-sabi* is where cracked pottery is filled with lacquer that has gold dust in it and actually highlights the crack, which makes this piece beautiful in its brokenness.

Lately, we have been focusing on the social-emotional health of our students, so doesn't it make sense that we should consider that in leading others? Some goals of social-emotional health are to improve self-control, to problem-solve, and to strengthen communication. Those three, especially the last two, are a huge part of our job as leaders.

Social-emotional health begins with safe relationships. Obviously, I realize the importance of building relationships, as I devoted an entire chapter to this trait. The other building blocks in this model are self-regulation, awareness of self, understanding others, and finally becoming a change-maker, or as I like to say, a *"Wave-Maker."* There is nothing in this model that should not be considered in leading your staff. If we want to teach the whole child, shouldn't we lead the whole adult as well?

I love to play golf. When I watch professional golfers, I am in awe of their skill in shot-making, their course management, and their focus. I notice how they finish and how they are rarely out of balance. I see them hit fades and draws, low and high shots, and make the ball stop and back up on the green. I see them recover from under trees, out of deep rough, and out of sand traps. What I don't see is the literal thousands of hours of practice that gets them to this level of play. They make it look so easy. My favorite golfer was Arnold Palmer. The reason I liked him so much was the way he showed emotion and how friendly he was around the fans. I remember sharing a huge issue with a fellow superintendent one day, and she told me, "Well, you made it look easy. They

don't understand the work and hours you put in to get there."
I got to thinking, is it our job to make it look easy? I got to
thinking about the jobs we have had, the books we read, the
conferences we attend, and the meetings we sit through get us
to where we are now. Maybe sometimes we should share how
we struggle before we get to our goal. Perhaps, we should
show our emotion more.

We must take off our armor (maybe ego?) of toughness and
knowing all the answers, and show our people that we have a
heart and emotions. We need to admit when we are wrong.
We need to ask for help. We all have fears (even though this
book is about being fearless). We are human, and the
unknown makes us uneasy and maybe a bit fearful. That is a
big reason why change is so hard. If we continue to strive to
build safe and healthy relationships and just simply love the
person in front of us, we will lead with significance.

Try to have empathy, just looking at the other perspective—
not your own (leader's) perspective, but that of those you are
leading. Try to understand how they feel. Practice mindful-
ness by just paying attention, noticing body language and eye
contact, noticing questions or comments, and listening—
really listening. Do not try to lead like someone you are not. It
will come out eventually anyway, so just be you. Sometimes
we need to forget about the four Ps - perform, perfect, prove,
and please. However, we should never forget our beliefs, principles, and ethics. I once had a parent tell me, "you walk your

talk. You get stuff done." If we do not walk our talk, we can never gain trust. If we cannot gain trust, we cannot influence. If we cannot influence, we cannot lead.

On this leg of our voyage, we load humility, which might be the heaviest. We definitely leave our comfort zone as we rumble with humility and vulnerability. We could play it safe and keep our boat tied up in the harbor. However, we all know ships are not made to stay in the harbor, they are made to sail! Make Waves!

EMPOWERING OTHERS IS REAL LEADERSHIP

We empower ourselves every time we accept responsibility for choosing thoughts and feelings we act on.—Karen Casey

Education is transformational and empowering. It literally changes lives. That is why people work so hard to become educated, and that is why education has always been the key to the American Dream, the force that erases arbitrary division of race and class and culture and unlocks every person's God-given potential. —Condoleezza Rice

Education is not a tool for development—individual, community, and the nation. It is the foundation for our future. It is empowerment to make choices and emboldens the youth to chase their dreams.—Nita Ambani

It is not about having power, but giving power to others. As I said in a previous chapter, when you use power, you lose power. You may not agree with me on this. But think about it: if you have to use your power to make a change, then use it again and again, eventually, you will lose your influence, and your crew will question instead of support you. Please understand there are times (as in the authority chapter) that you have to be the beast and use your roar, your power. However, make sure you have exhausted all other avenues before you do this.

I think you all will agree that you did not reach your leadership position alone. You had help, maybe even a mentor, to assist you in your leadership quest. That is exactly why I am suggesting that you empower those seeking a leadership position. Some may not think of themselves as a leader, but you can recognize one as you get to know your crew. I encourage you to seek those who are passionate about what they do and support and mentor them. Give them opportunities and watch them grow and become leaders.

There was once a time early in my career when I was taking classes to attain my M.Ed. —I was an athletic director and was considering going into campus administration. The classes sometimes required us to travel to the university campus, which was about ninety minutes away. As a result, I participated in a carpool with two others. As you might imagine, there were a plethora of different conversations, but mostly it had to do with our administrative jobs, future goals, and the direction in which we were all planning to go. I can vividly remember one time when I shared that I just really did not know what to do when I finished my classes. It was then that Jenny Preston told me, "Hal, you are having a hard time deciding, because you empower others wherever you are." This really shocked me! She eventually became a well-respected superintendent at a very large and fast-growing district in Texas. I never imagined that I could empower or inspire others, and still have a hard time accepting that.

As leaders, we need to listen to our teachers and show that we care and are enthusiastic about the job they do. The following report is alarming:

For people who have a heavy influence on the engagement of young people, you'd think teachers would be more engaged in their jobs. Yet nearly 7 in 10 are not emotionally connected to or are dissatisfied

with their workplaces, according to a 2014 Gallup
report. As part of its "State of America's Schools"
report released Wednesday, Gallup used the answers
of more than 7,000 teachers regarding various aspects
of their workplaces, including whether they know
what's expected of them at work, whether they have
the materials needed to do their jobs, and whether they
feel their supervisors or others at work care about them
as a person. (US News & World Report, online, April
9, 2014, "Most teachers are not engaged in their jobs—
Gallup finds")

You see, leadership is about *empowering* others, building
leaders, and leading collaboratively toward the vision set
forth. Our job is to influence others by gaining their trust, so
we are all sailing toward the same destination. Leadership is
not about a destination, but is, instead, a never-ending journey. There are always other ideas to explore, programs to
expand, ways to improve, and new crew members to hire. Our
job is to make our organization run smoothly when we are not
around—not that it cannot run without our daily input. Eventually, we are all replaced, and our goal should be that we are
replaced by a leader we have mentored along the way. One of
my PLN members and aspiring leader Sandy King
(@sandyteach) tells it this way:

Leaders build confidence in their followers because they believe in them. They trust that people will make good decisions, are there to coach and support, and let them learn through trial and error. My grandpa had a can-do attitude that was contagious. He built up our confidence by complimenting our abilities. He was excited by our desire to take some risks and head out on an adventure.

Great leaders do the same. They build trusting relationships and create positive changes. Their compliments are genuine and specific. They inspire individuals to discover, develop, and use their special gifts. Perhaps most importantly, great leaders affirm and validate people's worth by instilling in them a confidence and a belief in themselves. Challenges come, but people are confident that they can reach the ridge and climb even higher because their leader conveys a belief in their abilities and demonstrates a genuine appreciation for their efforts to take risks and grow.

President Truman had on his desk, "the buck stops here." We all know what that means, and as a leader, it always does; no matter how much collaboration you have, when it comes down to where your boss or board look for accountability, they will look at you. When we work together, those decisions tend to work out better with more success. In this long voyage of leadership, there is smoother sailing in reaching each destination along the way.

As my Twitter PLN member George Couros (@gcouros) says, "As leaders in education, our job is not to control those whom we serve but to unleash their talent." To unleash their talent, they need to have freedom in their classrooms. It is our mission to help our teachers become *fearless* teachers, teachers who have the freedom to try new ideas, projects, or pedagogy, and they know we are supportive of their efforts.

In this spirit, to *edify* means to improve the mind positively and to uplift a person. Each time you choose to edify your crew, they begin to appreciate and like you more, and that leads to more trust for you. Every chance you get, try to tell your followers that they are appreciated. I am not saying in a general meeting when they are all there, although this works some of the time; I am talking about short notes handwritten by you. E-mail is okay but just does not carry the weight of a note written by you. This is a dying practice that needs to be reborn! A written note is appreciated more because the recipient knows that you took the time to write, and they know they have worth to their leader and organization. Anytime you visit a classroom, take about five minutes, recognize something positive that you saw, and write a note to each teacher that you visit. I wonder how many of you have received in the mail a written letter or card with a handwritten note in it in the last month? Imagine what an impact it would have on you if you received one, unexpectedly.

Twitter friend Jonathan Kegler (@JonathanKegler) says this about the meaning of *edify*:

When one thinks about the term of "edifying," they must be prepared to build up others no matter what the circumstance or situation. I would say that in a school system, business, or any other walk of life, the act of edifying someone is more difficult than not acting at all or the fallback method of tearing them down. You see, many traditional leaders are title driven and seek to control the environment by keeping others in "their place."

However, we are here to look at the ultimate leader, and the chosen is the role of a servant-leader. You see, with a servant-leadership model, the leader exists to serve and assist the staff. This is in contrast from the title-driven, top-down approach described earlier. When in a leadership position, it is easy to uplift your staff by giving them words of encouragement, chances to utilize their talents, and opportunities to assist in the overall decision-making process. When you promote encouragement among your staff, the edifying is something that becomes contagious and begins to spread like wildfire. When you model allowing others to utilize their talents, you enable them to stretch their minds and further your company/organization.

The opportunity for growth becomes larger when you allow, encourage, and empower your staff to take risks and allow their talents to shine. The final segment of quality leadership that edifies and builds capacity among staff is to provide opportunities to take part in the decision-making process. The mark of a good leader is one that can build a culture of success that can continue even in their absence. To be able to do this, the decision-making process has to be shared among the staff, and all ideas/beliefs/questions have to be taken into account. When the leader does this, they edify others by establishing an environment that values input from all to come up with the best possible solution to any problem that exists. You see, a leader who consistently uses edifying of others becomes allergic to the statement, "we've always done it this way!" A true leader who wants to build the capacity of all parties involved must establish a system that has a center, core belief of edifying others. When you lower yourself and build up others, then at the end of the day, you will be lifted on the shoulders of the men and women that you have wisely chosen to edify.

I once taught a class created by the late Zig Ziglar and Mamie McCullough, called the "I Can Course." It called for students to speak in front of their classmates throughout the course. At the end of each "speech," the students and I would not only give them an ovation, but also write out on their "I like [student's name] because" notes to the student just finishing the talk. I would instruct them to be specific about at least one thing that they liked about that student's speech. I would collect them and, after reading (and checking for appropriateness), hand them back to the student the next day. At the end of the semester, they would have dozens of positive affirmations about them, just like notes that I would periodically receive (and still have to this day in a few folders) that would thank me for something. It is a way to remind people that they are appreciated.

I want to take a moment to talk about another *E* that is very important in reaching your crew—*emotion*. I have mentioned it briefly before, but you need to know the importance of emotion. Emotion is the gateway to the brain and cannot be controlled—just try to control your emotion when your doorbell rings in the middle of the night, or when you see the red lights of a police car in your rearview mirror. You can control the way you respond to emotion but cannot control the emotion itself, as it is like trying to stop a sneeze. Emotion causes the arousal of senses. It prepares the brain and the rest of the body for some kind of action.

Besides the initial response, emotion is also a means for focusing on reflection and action. I share this information because your job is to communicate a vision for your organization. If you cannot grab and keep the attention of your people, you will not engage them. You must remember, they will be engaged with something—you just need to make sure that they are engaged with your message. Emotion moves people to attention, judgment, and motivation. Isn't that what you are trying to do when you stand in front of a group?

So the three *Es* that I have discussed so far, all need to be included in your Wave-Making leadership voyage. We all should strive to empower others. This will be quite easy for some and quite difficult for others. If you are "old school" in your leadership philosophy, empowering will be quite difficult. I think we all have some "old school" in us—it is just a matter of how much and *if* or *when* we choose to migrate to a more collaborative style. I understand that one cannot lead in only one way, but we must use a plethora of styles to adapt to the crews and situations you must deal with daily.

The apostle Paul did an amazing job of empowering. You see, when you witness to others about the power of God, then He, in turn, will empower you to complete whatever mission, will, or journey He has in store for you. What a great promise that is for us! Paul took every opportunity to tell others, share his story, and show his love. The job of believers is to advance the kingdom. As we carry out this mission, God empowers us every step of the way. However, He wants us to walk by faith, as this scripture says, "Thy word is a lamp unto my feet, and a light unto my path" (Ps. 119:105). He just gives us enough light for us to walk a little way and does not provide a spotlight for us to see very far.

Empowerment baggage is one of the last pieces to load on our ship for our voyage. It is quite important, and definitely not to be left onshore. So let's load it up and get ready to set sail on our leadership mission. Make Waves!

MAKING WAVES!

Just think, when you are with a group of people on the same voyage as you, you begin to gain confidence. Once you see the destination, you begin to feel empowered. Pirates sought this. They wanted to escape the monotony. They were rebels against authority, free spirits to make their own laws and regulations. They wanted to sail the high seas for adventure.

However, I want to paint an accurate picture, as most pirates were in their late twenties, ex-seamen, and not aristocrats or educated men. The pirate captains were often mean and ruthless. More died a death by hanging or were carried away in a storm than were living the dream of pieces of eight and woman by his side.

All that said, sailing a ship on the open ocean, voyaging with a group of men (and maybe women) looking to obtain riches, was a very empowering experience.

14

LEAD TO SERVE

Always render more and better service than is expected of you, no matter what your task may be. —Og Mandino

Service to others is the rent you pay for your room here on earth.—Muhammad Ali

Earn your success based on the service to others, not at the expense of others.—H. Jackson Brown, Jr.

If service is below you, then leadership is beyond you.

Your gifts are not about you. Leadership is not about you. Your purpose is not about you. A life of significance is about serving those who need your gifts, your leadership, your purpose. —Kevin Hall

Striving to be a servant leader should be every leader's mission. It is through service that one gets totally fulfilled. When you can help someone who can do nothing in return, that is true service. Service starts with the love of others. Building positive relationships is the foundation upon which we build our leadership model. We should strive to love the people who are under our influence and authority. It is very difficult to serve your crew if you have not built a relationship with them. If you simply perform acts of service without a foundation of positive, healthy relationships, your people will see it as insincere or manipulative. Genuine concern is how you inspire loyalty among your followers. With a group of professionals under you, they will perform at their maximum potential when they feel cared for and loved by their leader.

My friend and PLN member Joe Clark (@DrJoeClark) says this:

_____

For me, my passion for leadership comes from a

philosophy that life is all about service to others. When I was a freshman in high school, I read the book *The Greatest Miracle in the World* by Og Mandino, and there is a quote that stuck out to me. In fact, I have this quote on my office wall and also give to all my new hires. This is it: "The surest way to doom yourself to mediocrity is to perform only work for which you are paid."

I love how it talks about being "doomed" to mediocrity. In other words, being mediocre is a curse, not a blessing. We are capable of greatness, and if we settle for mediocrity, we are living a life not worth living. Second, it speaks to the fact that if you don't want to be mediocre, you need to serve others. What honor is there in doing the work for which you are paid? There is none. Even the dregs of society work for their pay. True greatness comes from giving beyond what is expected of us.

As I have said earlier, it is the job of our teachers to not only teach content and curriculum, but more importantly, to enhance the lives of the students they teach. In turn, it is our job to enhance the lives of the people who follow us. It is critical to understand that unless we love our people, we may be tempted to use, sometimes neglect, and maybe even discard them.

It is vital to remember where we began our career. We were once new to the profession with no experience, striving to be noticed and wanting to matter. We need to remember what it is like to walk in those shoes. This is why it is so important to immerse yourself with your people and your organization.

One friend on Twitter who introduced me to educational chats, Kristal Floyd, (@KristalFloyd) wrote this about her passion for serving:

As I've been thinking about passion of leadership the last week, I wanted it to be something earth-shattering and my passion is really pretty simple. My passion in leadership is serving others. Being a leader has always been important to me, not because I want to be in the spotlight (which is really the farthest from what I want). My passion in leadership is to inspire others to greatness by serving them.

She helped me tremendously in introducing to me what Twitter has to offer. She even made a video to help my teachers set up their Twitter accounts. Kristal is a model of a servant leader.

One of my biggest faults as a leader was trying to please everyone. When I didn't, I took it very personally. If someone was not happy with a decision I made, I let it affect me. Occasionally, early in my leadership career, I would even change a decision just to try to please. I was once told that the best a leader could expect was to have 80 percent of your followers supporting them. Doing the math, 20 percent do not and probably will not support you. You will never make everyone happy. I think we should try, but not to take it personally if we cannot. If we adopt the mindset of a servant leader, we will get our fulfillment in service and not in trying to please.

The host of Twitter chat #ChristianEducators, Rik Rowe (@RoweRikW), says this regarding what it means to serve:

When we serve others, we honor and value them. When we tend to the needs of others, we demonstrate that we attribute worth to them. When we extend kindness, a listening ear, or an opportunity to share in a burden, we esteem worth to another, and others are often encouraged or inspired. I aim to keep myself as healthy as possible to take every opportunity to serve and encourage others. I believe everyone can serve others in some capacity.

To be a servant leader, one of our goals should be to inspire confidence. As we serve as their authority, we protect our followers, which results in the freedom to feel secure and safe. That is so important in feeling courageous to try new techniques, technology, and ideas. Isn't that what we want our teachers to feel?

The best picture of servant leadership is when Jesus chose to wash the feet of his disciples. You have to remember that washing someone's feet during this time in history was the ultimate in service. Their feet were filthy, calloused, and unkempt. He wanted to show them what it meant to lower oneself to serve, another example of what it takes to lead. He even washed the feet of Judas, knowing Judas would betray him just hours later.

In my first principal job, I served in a district that was somewhat small. The building I was in only had one custodian, and she worked during the school day. When she was sick, there were no substitutes. I just did what needed to be done, mopped the restrooms, picked up trash from classrooms, and swept the hallways. The secretary came to my office after the first time I did this and said that she had never seen that in any of the principals she had worked for. She had been in the district for over thirty years and had seen many principals come and go. With a big smile on her face, she said, "now that is service!" She even called the superintendent to tell him what I was doing. I just smiled and said that all those things needed to be done.

Paul continually showed what it was to serve. He was the perfect example of what it took to "die to self." He was even willing to die for his Lord in serving Him. When I think about what it means to serve, I think it is to put someone else's needs before mine. Jesus said it best when He was about to be crucified, talking to His disciples,

---

Anyone who intends to come with me has to let me lead. You're not in the driver's seat; I am. Don't run from suffering; embrace it. Follow me and I'll show you how. Self–help is no help at all. Self–sacrifice is the way, my way, to finding yourself, your true self (Matt. 16:24–26, MSG).

Service could very well be the lightest piece of cargo we load to our vessel. It is light because we just need to take the first step in serving, and after that first step, it begins to get easier. However, it could also be quite heavy because it takes time and effort and to put self-interest out of the way and put others' needs ahead of ours. So you must decide, are you in this for pride of self, or pride for others? Let's load service onto our ship and do what is best for others and students. Make Waves!

MAKING WAVES!

If serving is below you, then leadership is beyond you. You must move from self-centered (which is often a natural tendency), and move to others-centered. Thinking of others first is the heart of servant leadership. The problem is, this kind of thinking is unnatural, counter-cultural, rare, and difficult.

The first responsibility of a leader is to define reality. The last is to say thank you. In between, the leader must become a servant.—Max Dupree

Service is the pathway to real significance.

15

WE MUST BE KINDLERS OF HOPE

Hope is being able to see that there is light despite all of the darkness. —Desmond Tutu

A leader is a dealer in hope.—Napoleon

A good teacher can inspire hope, ignite the imagination, and instill a love of learning.—Brad Henry

Since we have such a hope, we are very bold.—2 Corinthians 3:12 (NIV)

Optimism is the faith that leads to achievement.

Nothing can be done without hope and confidence.—Helen Keller

I believe that imagination is stronger than knowledge. That myth is more potent than history. That dreams are more powerful than facts. That hope always triumphs over experience. That laughter is the only cure for grief. And I believe that love is stronger than death. —Robert Fulghum, *All I Really Need to Know I Learned in Kindergarten: Uncommon Thoughts On Common Things*

Some of our students are hemorrhaging hope! I believe that ultimately, it is our job to kindle hope. We should strive to change the odds to change our students' trajectories in a positive upward path. We must be merchants of hope! We should strive to make hope building pervasive for every student, every day, and in every period. Regarding hope, Barack Obama might have said it best,

I'm not talking about blind optimism, the kind of hope that just ignores the enormity of the tasks ahead or the roadblocks that stand in our path. I'm not talking about the wishful idealism that allows us to just sit on the sidelines or shirk from a fight. I have always believed that hope is that stubborn thing inside us that insists, despite all the evidence to the contrary, that something better awaits us so long as we have the courage to keep reaching, to keep working, to keep fighting.

The 2017 Student Gallup Poll says this about hope:

Hopeful students are 2.8x more likely to say they get better grades than their discouraged peers. Hope: The ideas and energy students have for the future. Hope has also been linked to student success in school. Hopeful students are positive about the future, goal-oriented and can overcome obstacles in the learning process, enabling them to navigate a pathway to achieve their goals.

Gallup measures three constructs (hope, engagement, well-being). Gallup measures these three because their research shows these metrics account for one-third of the variance of student success. Yet schools do not measure these things. **Hope is a better predictor of student success than SAT scores, ACT scores, and grade point average.**

Among the 808,521 Gallup (2017) Student Poll participants, 38% STRONGLY AGREE that the adults at school care about them. Of students who participated in 2017, 4 in 10 students STRONGLY AGREE they feel safe in their school!

Dr. Amy Fast (@fastcrayon) an Assistant Principal at McMinnville High School in Oregon, recently tweeted,

---

> Our school is a high poverty school. And thus, many of our kids face more than I can imagine. Yet, they constantly outperform districts around the state on traditional measures. It can't be a coincidence that the % of students who indicate they're hopeful is also off the charts.

You see, our students are not looking for miracles; they are looking for hope. They only get that when they struggle and make a choice to keep going. We need to help them make that choice — to persevere when adversity is in their lives. Brené Brown, author of *Dare to Lead,* says, "...hope is not an emotion but rather a behavioral process born from overcoming adversity — a habit of mind founded in resilience." So when we talk about fostering hope in our classes and schools, we should not mistake that with making everything easy or running away from struggle. Hope is not a soft nebulous option; it is what we do inside ourselves, the inner work of clearing the disappointment, fear, and hopelessness, choosing hope over despair, and making an effort when it feels the hopelessness creeping in. Kindling hope in our students gives them resilience; provides for positive, healthy, safe relationships; and gives them optimism. We have to heal the soul before we can move into improving performance. The only way to heal the soul is through intentional relationships and authentic love.

We are called to create a culture where students have the freedom to take off the heavy weight of their armor as they walk in our door and open their heart. At the same time, we must protect that freedom where they can be curious, put the *awe* back in awesome, be themselves without that armor, and be allowed to breathe freely. They should feel safe to open their hearts in a place and space to belong, where we show them that they matter. This is when hope changes the trajectory of their path.

Hope is the belief that our tomorrows can be better than our todays. Hope is not magic; hope is work.

In my initial faculty meeting as principal of two high schools and at a district convocation when I was superintendent, I made a point of saying, "I believe in the three As of education: advanced academics, arts, and athletics." These three provide a balanced curriculum, much like a three-legged stool. If you take away one of those, then it is out of balance and will not stand. In almost every high performing school, high expectations (no matter the demographics) include a complex, challenging curriculum including arts (performing, musical, and media), athletics (including as many sports as possible), and advanced academic classes. Also, leaders add support to each student who needs it. A great example of this kind of support is AVID (Advancement Via Individual Determination), a college readiness system for students in kindergarten through 12th grade. AVID provides a curriculum that includes Writing, Inquiry, Collaboration, Organization, and Reading (WICOR) strategies to help students become college-ready. AVID also provides teacher training in every subject, enhancing the college-going culture of the school.

When you teach the whole child (mind, body, and spirit), you help him obtain hope. If you take away any one of these, you are cheating the student. This includes free play at recess when kids learn creativity in making up games, as well as how to fend for themselves. The arts and a rigorous curriculum enhance learning skills and cognition. Athletics, recess, and physical education classes help the brain grow neurons (neurogenesis) and decrease depression. Therefore, every school should include athletics and physical activity, arts, and advanced academic curriculum in *every* school day. This curriculum is in addition to any gifted & talented program that might be in place. A rigorous curriculum is needed for *every* student.

Hope is the inner fire that warms us, the inner light that gives us direction, the fuel that gives us the energy to keep moving forward. It is born out of meaning and purpose and, in turn, creates meaning in our lives. Hope is a powerful force that can change the trajectory of each student that it touches. For me, it's simple. For students to achieve success (no matter how they define it), they need just one thing: *hope*! It is hope that will energize them, drive them forward, encourage them, and give them the strength and courage to keep moving.

Let me return to my analogy of Dorothy in *The Wizard of* Oz, and of her three companions as they collaborate to defeat an enemy and reach their goal. Dorothy found out what each three were lacking and created a way to give each one hope that one day, they could own it. Once they had hope, they were able to persevere through several hurdles to obtain what they were lacking. Hope is powerful!

I am inclined to think that hope originates with love. The most important things I looked for when I was interviewing educators was if they loved kids — *all* kids. I believe that this love is a choice. It reminds me of Who I believe is the greatest teacher and leader and how He addressed love. His some followers asked, "Teacher, which is the greatest commandment in the Law?" Jesus replied,

'Love the Lord your God with all your heart and with all your soul and with all your mind.' This is the first and greatest commandment. And the second is like it, 'Love your neighbor as yourself.' All the Law and the Prophets hang on these two commandments (Matthew 22: 36-39 NIV).

I find it interesting that *neighbor* is not defined here. I believe this was intentional so that we could not qualify who our neighbor is. Isn't it a huge relief that we do not have to create a list of who our neighbor is and maybe more importantly, who we do *not* have to love? You see, we are commanded to love both the lovable and unlovable, the smart and the not-so-smart, the clean and the dirty, the athlete, thespian, band member, the black, brown, white, and all color of kids. Simply put — just love the one in front of you. Our school is a neighborhood. Mr. Rogers said, or should I say sang, it best.

> *It's a beautiful day in this neighborhood,*
> *A beautiful day for a neighbor,*
> *Would you be mine? Could you be mine?*
> *It's a neighborly day in this beautywood,*
> *A neighborly day for a beauty,*
> *Would you be mine? Could you be mine?*

*I have always wanted to have a neighbor just
    like you,
I've always wanted to live in a neighborhood
    with you.
So let's make the most of this beautiful day,
Since we're together, we might as well say,
Would you be mine? Could you be mine?
Won't you be my neighbor?
Won't you please, won't you please,
Please, won't you be my neighbor?[1]*

In one of my presentations, I use Walt Disney World and
Disneyland great examples of culture. The motto for Walt
Disney World is "The Most Magical Place on Earth," and the
motto for Disneyland is "The Happiest Place on Earth." If we
have a culture of happiness or magic, we will kindle hope and
give love. A classroom or campus where a student feels
magical or happy will experience hope and love every day.
Let's try to have that kind of culture in every classroom, every
period, for each child. Make Waves!

MAKING WAVES!

Hope is quite a heavy load, since some of our kids may not
have much. We have to change their mindset. So many expe-

rience some kind of trauma at home, so we must help them overcome that. Let's load plenty of hope so our kids can reach their potential.

---

1. Please won't you be my neighbor?" - *Won't You Be My Neighbor* by Fred M. Rogers. © The McFeely-Rogers Foundation

16

AIM FOR SIGNIFICANCE OVER GREATNESS

When value is added to you—it is greatness. When you add value to others—it is significance. —John Maxwell

What counts in life is not the mere fact that we have lived. It is what difference we have made to the lives of others that will determine the significance of the life we lead.—Nelson Mandela

What will matter in the end is not your success, but your significance.

God calls us to not be successful, but to be signif-

icant. When we focus on significance, success is often part of the package.—Tom Ziglar

I like to aim for significance over success because often can you be significant and also successful, but many people can be successful and not significant.—Alyson Stoner

As leaders, we strive for influence. There is nothing quite like realizing you have influenced your followers for the betterment of the organization. Ultimately, we want to be known as a leader of significance. It is perfectly okay to endeavor to be known as a great leader. In fact, shouldn't that be a goal of every leader?

Dave Burgess says, "Mediocrity doesn't inspire. Seeking greatness is a journey that can ignite, stoke, and continuously fuel a raging inferno." Notice that he says that greatness is a journey; it is never a destination. That is why we must persevere in good and bad times. I will refer you to the first sentence on one of the chapters of this book. "Leadership is hard." Nobody ever said that leadership will be easy, but it will be fulfilling when you realize you have made an impact on those you serve. And you must continually realize that your impact and dominion of influence is bigger than when you were a teacher. As I have said, leadership is never-ending, as we are continually learning, inspiring our followers, and seeking the next best practice that will improve our organization. We can never be satisfied to keep the status quo if we want to rise to lead with significance.

We are like professional athletes—we want the ring! I was fortunate to play for some successful teams. As a football Cardinal, we won the Eastern Conference of the N.F.L. As we entered our dressing room the first week of the playoffs, the first thing we saw was a drawing of a Super Bowl ring with the Cardinal logo at the top. That gave us a mental picture of what we had set out at the beginning of the year to win. That is the reason I would give my staff a lapel pin with the theme for the year on it. In education, we all have goals of exemplary scores, high SAT/ACT scores, graduation rates, and more. Sometimes, our goals are not as easily recognized as scores, but all the same, we and our crew should always have those goals on our minds for a successful year.

If you think about it: greatness or significance is a matter of making an impact on those we serve. You may be thinking that this goes against the previous chapter on serving. However, authentic significance actually fulfills the definition of servanthood. A truly great leader seeks first to serve, and everything else comes second. You see, I believe that God is not opposed to you striving to become great or significant. It is pride that He opposes. It is pride that your followers will not admire. I am not referring to having pride in the accomplishments of your crew or organization as a whole—it is the pride of self and a "look at me" attitude that I am referring to.

In Genesis, God promised Abraham that He would make his name great. Jesus said in John 14:12, "Truly, truly, I say to you, he who believes in Me, the works that I do, he will also do; and greater works than these he will do." This means God chooses the average, the humble, and the unlikely to make great. If you look at the great leaders in Scripture, probably none would have been chosen by worldly standards. You just have to be willing to be molded into the leader He needs to serve in His Kingdom. I think He searches for leaders like you to make an impact, to influence, and to enhance others' lives. He desires leaders like you to influence and impact your followers. In the Old Testament, Jeremiah used the term *clay* to describe what the Master Potter molds into what He chooses to make us. "Behold, like the clay in the potter's hand, so are you in My hand" (Jer. 18:6).

As you reflect on all of the previous attributes that I have written about in this book and start to internalize them, each one will help you emerge as a leader of significance. President Harry Truman once said, "A great leader is one who gets his followers to do something they do not want to do and like it." He does this by making a difference and enhancing their lives.

You are in the position of leadership because you are the best person for the job. You were chosen because you stood out among other candidates. It is no accident that you are serving in this leadership job. If you have been in the same position for some time, it means that you are accomplishing great things and continuing to impact your crew. As a result, they are performing the way you wanted when you delivered your vision.

As I close this book on *Wave Making* leadership, I want to remind you of what serving as a leader is all about.

- *What is Your Passion?* When you lead with passion, your crew starts to catch that passion as well. Passion is contagious. Passion for leading is critical to your success as a leader.
- *You Must Have Perseverance.* You will have some challenges in your job. Sometimes, those challenges take some time to solve. Never take those challenges in a personal way. I like to say, "keep on keeping on" toward your next objective. Your leadership voyage will often have rough waters. You just have to adjust your sails and continue the voyage.
- *Drench Yourself in Your Job.* We all know that we must immerse ourselves in our organization and community. That is the only way to build positive relationships. As a result, your crew gets to know you and allows them to see that they are important and that they matter. Immersion will help smooth the waters and make your cruise much easier.
- *There Is No Such Thing as a Minor Lapse of*

Integrity. Integrity is the cornerstone of a great leader. This attribute is critical for your success. Your crew should never be in doubt of your honesty, character, or ethics. Integrity should always be a part of every decision you make. Remember that your integrity takes time to build, but only a minute to lose.

- *Build Safe & Healthy Relationships.* Building positive relationships should be your priority throughout your career. This is the foundation that must always be nurtured. Neuroscience research says that building positive relationships opens the brain to learning, engagement, and influence. The brain continually seeks relationships as we are relational beings. This may be the most important attribute of a great leader.

- *"Assessment" is Not a Bad Word.* Never stop asking questions. Questions and analysis of the answers to those questions are where growth happens. No matter where you are in your journey, the success of your organization, or place in your vision, continue to ask questions and analyze every aspect of your organization. That is the job that every exceptional leader does.

- *Authority: The Buck Stops on Your Desk.* The buck will always stop on your desk. It is your job to protect and serve your crew. When your staff makes a poor decision, it is your job to make them accountable. Sometimes you have to use your "roar" to establish your dominion and to be the beast. Just make sure you do not have to do that too many times!

- *Change Is Hard.* You were not hired to maintain the status quo. My good friend, former principal of Bettendorf High School and author of three books, Jimmy Casas achieved the Bammy Educators Voice Award as the Secondary School Principal of the Year in 2014. Also in 2014, Jimmy was invited to the White House to speak on the Future Ready Schools pledge. He writes:

As school leaders, it is our responsibility to not allow average to become our standard. More than ever, I am convinced of one thing—leadership matters. It matters a lot. The longer I stay in the trenches as a school leader, the more I understand the difference between now and tomorrow is me. It's as simple as that. As principal, it is not only my responsibility to identify where average lives, but I have an obligation to make sure I am taking action to change it, not just manage it. You be the change, don't wait for someone else to make it happen.

- *Trust Is Never Owned.* If your crew does not like you, they will not trust you, and if they do not trust you, they will not follow you. Trust and integrity always go together, as you cannot have one without the other. Trust + relationships = influence, and that is where leadership happens.
- *Magic In Enthusiasm.* Enthusiasm lights the fire of your followers. It is contagious, just like passion. You can fake enthusiasm, and sometimes it is just necessary to do that. Any time you are in front of your staff, you should be enthusiastic. Maybe you should remember this quote, "If you are not fired up with enthusiasm, you will be fired with enthusiasm!"
- *Empowering is Real Leadership.* If you not empowering your followers, getting the most of their potential, and developing leaders, you are not accomplishing what exemplary leaders do. You must protect to empower. Let them have the freedom to fail when trying new and cutting-edge practices. There will be failure, but that is where the growth happens. Help and show them how to have success the next time they try it, and you will have a loyal follower.
- *Strive to Service.* You will never experience full joy and fulfillment until you are a servant leader. When you begin to put others' needs before yours, you will

want to continue serving. When you do something for someone who cannot return the favor, that is true service.

- *Aim For Significance.* This is what this book is all about—to be a leader of significance. Oliver Wendell Holmes says this, "I find the great thing in this world is not so much where we stand, as in what direction we are moving—we must sometimes sail with the wind and sometimes against it—but we must sail, and not drift nor lie at anchor."

- *Kindle Hope.* We need to build a culture of hope in our schools. Every period of every day, the goal of kindling hope should be on every teacher's mind. If you have a large population of kids living in poverty, this is vitally important. Many times these kids come to school with little hope. We all should work on providing better tomorrows and possibilities for each student we teach.

- *We Are Called to Produce Fruit.* Our job is to produce sweet-tasting fruit. We should strive to prepare, cultivate, fertilize, prune, and lift up so our "grapes" can thrive. We should help them crawl, then cling to their strong support team, so that they climb to reach their highest potential, and finally cluster to mature.

- *Humility Is Showing Vulnerability.* In today's world, it is almost unnatural for leaders to exhibit humility.

I believe this is because it makes you vulnerable. But the neat thing about this is that if you stay humble, your people with be drawn to you. You can cultivate more and deeper, positive relationships. People will work wonders for leaders that they like and trust.

When thinking of how to emerge as a leader of significance, I want to include a quote of one of the most inspiring speakers/authors of all time. The late Zig Ziglar said: "you can have anything you want in life if you just help enough other people get what they want." Always choose to heal, not to hurt, to forgive not to despise, to persevere not to quit, to smile not to frown, and to love not to hate. In the end, what really matters is not what we bought but what we built; not what we got but what we shared; not our competence but our character, and not our success but our significance. Live a life that matters. Life a life of adding value to others.

This is the last piece of cargo we must load onto our *Wave-Making* vessel. Striving for significance is something I probably did not need to include in this book but wanted to inspire you to greatness. This piece of cargo is almost weightless since it will lift you up and will tell you that, in fact, you have made a difference and enhanced the lives of the people you lead. Make Waves!

MAKING WAVES!

There are four questions that every follower asks of a leader:

1. Do you like me?
2. Can/will you help me?
3. Can I trust you?
4. Will you add value to my life/profession?

If you can answer with an emphatic "yes!" you will emerge as a leader of significance. Life is a series of choices or tests. How you invest your *time,* value your *resources,* use your *talents,* and value your *relationships* will determine your destiny. How you think usually determines your feelings and your feelings usually determine your actions.

Remember that everyone has five needs:

1. A *purpose* to live for — passion/service
2. *People* to live for — relationships
3. *Principles* to live by — integrity
4. *Profession* to live out —vision/mission
5. *Power* to live on & guide you — faith[1]

Always remember, as a leader, there are two keys to success & significance:

1. Never tell everything you know

2. ...

EVERY DAY MATTERS in education.

Now go and *MAKE WAVES!*

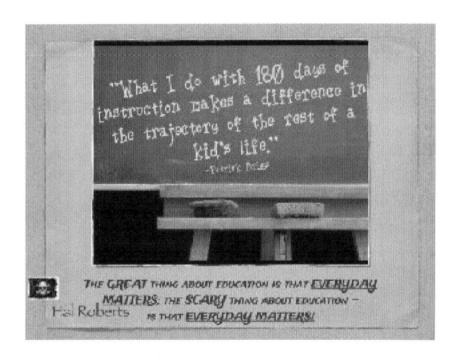

---

1. —Rick Warren from *A Purpose Driven Life*

AFTERWORD

When I received the edits from the publisher of my first book, I was entering one of the deepest valleys of my life. It might have been the lowest I have ever been. However, I have witnessed how  God worked before and continues to work in my life. There was not a time that God looked at my situation and said, "Hmmm...I did not see this coming!" He began to prepare me even before and has since placed fellow believers in my wife's and my path to love, encourage, and edify us in our darkest hours. He continues to work even as I am typing these words. Referring to what I wrote in the "Authority" chapter, it was as if God himself was holding up His three fingers letting me know, "I got this!"

I say this to encourage you to internalize the attributes, values, and qualities of leadership that I write about and apply them in your daily life, not just in leadership. Each of these should be a way that you live each day of your life, especially in your relationship with your loved ones and our Lord.

CONCLUSION

Teaching: Sometimes it seems deceptively simple; but you will find at times endlessly complicated; it  *will satisfy your soul and frustrate your intellect. It is at the same time rewarding and maddening— and it is without a doubt, the GREATEST profession mankind has ever known.*

(adapted from what Arnold Palmer said about golf that I edited/changed to fit teaching/education)

Every act you make today strikes a chord that will vibrate in eternity.—Edwin Hubbell Chapin

Leaders take people from here to there—what is your there?

To me, there are three things we all should do every day. We should do this every day of our lives. Number one is laugh. You should laugh every day. Number two is think. You should spend some time in thought. And number three is, you should have your emotions moved to tears, could be happiness or joy. But think about it. If you laugh, you think, and you cry, that's a full day. That's a heck of a day. You do that seven days a week, you're going to have something special.—Jimmy Valvano

I'm not interested if you've stood with the great. I'm interested if you've sat with the broken.

We are all neurocardiologists and neurosculptors —we touch the heart and mind, and we shape the young brains under our care every day.

Don't let the past determine your future. Avoid the dreaded TTWWADI—That's The Way We Always Did It!

Be a voice—not an echo.

Remember, we must satisfy Maslow before we can start on Bloom's.

As I close *Make Waves!*, I want you to remember that you are the captain of your ship (whatever that may be...a school, team, classroom, company, or organization). I want you to be intentional every day. All sailing vessels have some kind of guiding rudder. Never put your vessel on autopilot. As my favorite author and speaker, the late Zig Ziglar said, "Be a meaningful specific, not a wandering generality." Try to plan every hour of your day so that each day, you can accomplish everything you desire. Make it a goal to accomplish three things for that day.

I know in leadership, there are often interruptions that you must handle when those issues cross your desk. However, you must "stay the course" on your mission. I believe most leaders would agree that the most productive part of his/her day is before everyone arrives and after everyone leaves. I ask that you write in a journal after each day what you accomplished, how you added value to someone, and what you missed or did not finish, regarding what you set out to do that day. This practice will help you be accountable for your mission. I encourage you to set forth your team's core values that will guide in every decision you make. In this book, I have described 16 core values that your team could adopt. You might want to narrow to only a few, like the United States Marines whose core values are honor, courage, and commitment. Whatever you and your team decide, make the commitment to follow through with them! Make them non-negotiable!

For those who watch "Game of Thrones," I thought I would use Daenerys Targaryen for a good quote: "I survived because the fire inside me burned brighter than the fire around me!" She was fierce, focused, and fearless. I quote this for leading fearlessly. Make sure your fire burns brighter than any fire around you.

I lived on the Texas Gulf Coast for 20 of my 38 years in education. I had the opportunity to go into the Gulf on many occasions to fish. As we took our vessel out to the open waters, we first had to sail away and pass through a "No Wake Zone" where we had to go at a languid pace not to make waves where other boats are harbored. You see, this would create a safety issue to all the other vessels. I do not want you to cause trouble, especially that which affects the course of a situation in a negative way. What I am asking is that you *Make Waves!*, take some risks, and do something innovative that draws a large amount of attention and makes a widespread impact. You might cause a small bit of controversy, but in the end, you may create something that adds value to others. If you can commit to these attributes, you will *emerge as a leader of significance.*

I believe some of us in education have fallen guilty of "preparing the path for the student, not preparing the student for the path," just as I have witnessed the evolving trend moving from helicopter parents to lawnmower parents. I think we should help students prepare for landing if they fail. As I just typed those words, I believe that this counsel is good for leaders as well.

I have mentioned several times in this book to lead fearlessly. You may be thinking, *this is easy for you to say, Hal— you received a college scholarship, played in the N.F.L., obtained an athletic director job, served as an elementary and high school principal, climbed the administrative ladder to become an assistant superintendent, and eventually a superintendent. You were fortunate enough to create a high school and pass a bond to build it. Look at all your accomplishments!* Maybe I should have shared more about the hours I spent by myself punting footballs. Or I should have shared how many applications and interviews I had for each of those positions before I won the job. Or maybe I should have talked about getting cut from my eighth-grade football team, or getting placed on waivers three times in my professional football career. You see, I did fail many, many times! So we should learn for ourselves as professional educators to fail forward. I remember teaching my football players how to tumble and roll after being knocked down so that it became an automatic skill to bounce up from the ground. We should learn and teach those skills in life. You see, if we don't know and teach these skills, we (and they) may never take a risk.

There would be times that I would tell my secretary that I was going to take a walk when the stresses of my job would overwhelm me. I would then go outside (leave my cell phone on my desk) to feel the sun, experience the breeze—just be. I sometimes say, we are human beings, not human doings. Take some time to enjoy what God has created.

I was walking on a golf course with a fellow coach when we passed by some beautiful azalea bushes. We both commented on how pretty they were. I then said, "I bet our golfers don't even notice them." We both chuckled at that realizing they are focused on their golf game and not noticing the beauty all around them. I believe that sometimes we are guilty of getting so focused on our job, we do not take the time to notice the beauty that surrounds us. Remember that you cannot pour from an empty cup.

I have experienced the value of grace many times in my life. Even if you are not a spiritual person, you should understand what grace is. I will tell you that the one who benefits the most is the one who extends, grants, or gives it. Grace and forgiveness are not feelings—they are a choice. It is not about forgetting; it is just not making a repayment part of the deal. Grace and forgiveness are not the absence of consequences. It only has limited benefit to the one who caused the pain or misdeed. Consequences may happen. Grace is a gift that you give yourself. So try to make extending grace part of what you do as a leader.

Twenty years from now you will be more disappointed by the things you didn't do than by the things you did do. So throw off the bowlines. Sail away from safe harbor. Catch the trade winds in your sails. Explore. Dream. Discover. To revisit how we ended the Introduction: explore *His* will, dream *His* dreams, and discover *His* purpose for you.

Make Waves!

APPENDIX

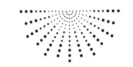

THE "UMAMI" LESSON PLAN

A.K.A. THE PERFECT LESSON PLAN

Umami is synonymous with the taste of perfection—a glass of wine at its apex of flavor maturity and quality. Linguists have suggested that Umami (pronounced oo-mom´-ee) has English equivalents, such as savory, essence, deliciousness...Umami is associated with an experience of perfect quality in taste. It is also said to involve all the senses, not just that of taste. In the Asian context, there is both a spiritual and mystical quality to Umami. In the West, it has been controversial whether it involves all the senses, not just that of taste. In wine, Umami is said to have *depth* and *complexity*. Karen MacNeil author of *The Wine Bible* says this about wine, "I talk about the following as hallmarks of greatness: Distinctiveness, Precision, Balance, Complexity, Connectedness, Choreography, Length, and the Ability to Evoke an Emotional Response."

Are you beginning to see where I'm going with this? Maybe a great lesson should have these hallmarks?

The illustration I have provided is a slide in my presentation entitled, "The Neurocardiologist Teacher/Leader," where I tell my participants that this is the *template* for a perfect lesson plan for *any* grade and *any* subject. I have also developed a presentation specifically on developing a perfect lesson plan.

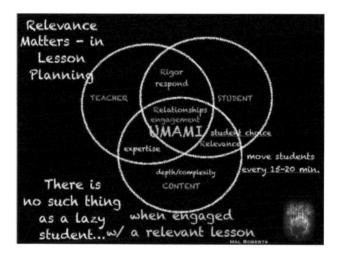

There are three main components to this lesson plan: *teacher, student,* and *content.*

All three *must intersect* for that perfect plan to happen. Each touches the other in different but fundamental ways. Included in the circles are *rigor, relevance,* and *relationships.*

Although there are many presentations, frameworks, conferences, and more on *rigor, relevance,* and *relationships,* you will see that mine is quite simple and easy to understand.

It all begins with the *teacher* developing positive *relationships* with her students. One summer, I heard Victor Mendoza, an AVID graduate of McKinney High School in McKinney, Texas, chosen to speak at the Dallas AVID Summer Institute. He said that there is an "emptiness or a gray area" between the student and teacher until that teacher develops a healthy and positive relationship with him. I cannot stress enough the importance of this foundation as it is THE most critical piece. Neuroscience supports this, as the brain continually seeks relationships. Until the brain finds a positive relationship, long-term memory will be difficult and possibly will never take place.

The next important piece is the *relevance* of the lesson. I have it intersected with the student as it must be relevant to him, so he connects the content to himself. It is vitally important for the teacher to know as much about each student as possible—even the cultural roots of her students. These roots determine how one makes sense of the world. It is the software for the brain's hardware. It is imperative that the teacher bridges the cultural divides before she delivers content.

The teacher should strive to share stories in her presentation of the objective, as the brain loves a good story. Stories touch the emotions and emotions are the gateways to the brain and learning. Also included in that intersection is student *choice*. Sometimes it is not possible/feasible to allow students to have a *choice* of content, but the teacher should always look for this possibility as it provides ownership to the learner and adds to the Umami lesson. Designing your classroom to have flexible seating (getting rid of "cemetery rows") is an excellent way for students to have a *choice*. In the content circle is *depth/complexity*. *Rigor*, though all educators understand this term, lately has been given a bad rap (at least on Twitter). So I choose depth and *complexity* to the content/objective (this also aligns with my Umami example). The bottom line is to rise above knowledge and comprehension of Bloom's. I use another slide to compare *depth/complexity* to difficulty. I will not delve into that in this article, but in short, *depth/complexity/rigor* is NOT "more" and is not the same as "difficult!"

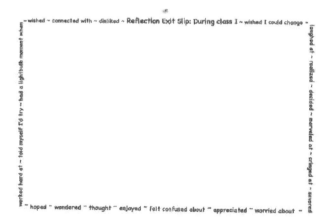

I kept *rigor* in the intersection between the student and teacher for how the teacher questions the students when she checks for understanding. I have attached a couple of examples to formatively assess your students. An exit slip for students to fill out after the lesson is a way to assess during a lesson. Maybe, more importantly, the teacher should strive to move her students above knowledge/comprehension, above level one on Costa's, and preferably to level three or four in Webb's Depth of Knowledge. *Complexity* begins with the level of questions posed by the teacher. Using Costa's Levels of Inquiry is an essential piece of this lesson plan. Go above Level One and teach your students to recognize the different levels of questions to enhance their learning. The teacher must be intentional about her questions to make students think, not just regurgitate information. We must move from a culture of consumption to one of creation. In this same intersection is *respond,* a time for students to *respond* to the teacher about the objective (preferably in some form of writing). This is an excellent way to formatively assess the level of understanding and application to the objective.

The teacher should have expertise in the subject, objective(s), standards—the content included in the lesson. I am not saying that she has all the answers, but the teacher should have a deep understanding and ability to lead students to higher-level thinking as I have discussed above.

In the middle, where all three intersect are three words: *rela-*

tionships, engagement, and *Umami. Relationships* are not just between the teacher and student (although the most important) but also between the student and the content. The learner must have that relationship for the lesson to reach the Umami level. The second is *engagement.* Students will find something with which to engage. Every student is engaged! They may or may not be engaged in the teacher's lesson, but they are engaged in something. This plan will ensure that the learner is engaged in the teacher's objective.

Quick and Easy
Formative Assesssments

Assessments FOR learning happens while learning is still underway.

Hand Signals	Ask students to display a designated hand signal to indicate their understanding of a specific concept, principal or process. Thumbs Up or Thumbs down, 5 Fingers 1-5 scale
Index Card	Distribute index cards and ask students to write on both sides, with these instructions. Side 1: Based on our study of _____, list a big idea that you understand. Side 2 Identify something about _____ that you do not yet fully understand.
One Minute Essay	A one-minute essay question is a focused question with a specific goal that can, in fact, be answered within a minute or two.
Analogy Prompt	Present students with a an analogy prompt: A designated concept, principal or process is like _____ because _____ Analogies are a great way to assess what your student know in a fun way.
Concept Map	Any of several forms of graphical organizers with allow learns to perceive relationships between concepts through diagramming key words representing these concepts. Http://www.graphic.org/concept.html
"Brain Dumps" 3 minute Pause Or Turn to your partner	The 3-minute pause provides a chance for students to stop, reflect on the concepts and ideas that have just been introduced, make connections to prior knowledge or experience, and seek clarification. • I changed my attitude about... • I became more aware of ... • I was surprised about ... • I felt... • I related to ... • I empathized with... • This reminds me of ... (Text to text, text to world, text to self) • I can adapt ...
Exit Card	Exit Cards are written student responses to questions posed at the end of a class or learning activity or at the end of the day.
Journal Entry	Students record in their journal their understanding of the topic, concept or lesson taught. The teacher reviews the entry to see if the student has grained an understanding of the topic, lesson or concept that was taught.

The one thing I didn't include in the three circles is *movement*. Body cognition shows that the brain actually learns from the body. You must have some kind of *movement* or brain breaks. Get students to move! In a 45-55 minute lesson, there should be at least two brain breaks where students should get out of their desks and move. "The greater duration in the chair, the greater depth of student despair." —Eric Jensen, author of many neuroscience books

In this presentation, I first ask the question, "How many of you believe there is no such thing as a lazy student?" I never get 100% until I add, "when *engaged* with a *relevant* lesson?" At that point, I get close to 100% agreement. If the teacher includes all of the attributes I have outlined, she will have an Umami lesson, a lesson that has "*depth* and *complexity*, a taste of perfection, the apex of flavor maturity and quality, a deliciousness..." What teacher does not want that? What student does not want that?!

THE PERFECT LESSON PLAN TEMPLATE

Name _____

Date: _____

Subject:_____

Unit: _____

Greeting: Classroom: Music/Song; YouTube video...
Door: Handshake; fist bump: high five...

Lesson Topic: _____
(Can I create an experience?)
(Can I flip this lesson?)
(Is there a story to tell? Emotion to touch?)
(How can I use images/colors?)
(How can I make them "struggle thinkers?")

(Remember cultural roots "lenses.")
(Meet Maslow first!)
(What is the gist?)

Student Choice?
Options:_____
http://shar.es/1oWNiA

Relevance:_____

Standard(s):

_____

_____

_____

Hook/Bell ringer activity:

_____

Focus/Essential Question(s) for Rigor:
(Level on Bloom's Taxonomy; Marzano's Taxonomy; Costa's
Level of Inquiry; Webb's DOK)
(Prior knowledge/Review; Predict?)

_____

_____

_____

Formative Assessment:

Digital Hard Copy

Technology:

Movement/Brain Breaks:

Student Written Response Activity:

MOVE YOUR STUDENTS FROM
CONSUMPTION TO CREATION

KINDLE HOPE. CREATE HEALTHY
RELATIONSHIPS. USE BRAIN-FRIENDLY
STRATEGIES.

You are a Neurosculptor & Neurocardiologist!

RIGOR

New Bloom's Taxonomy | *Marzano's Taxonomy*

Remembering

Retrieval | recognizing, recalling, executing

Understanding

Comprehension | integrating, symbolizing

Applying

Analysis | *matching, classifying, analyzing errors,*
Analyzing

generalizing, specifying

Evaluating

Knowledge Utilization | *decision making, problem*

Creating

solving, experimenting, investigating

WEBB'S DEPTH OF KNOWLEDGE

Recall & Reproduction

Recall a fact, information, or procedure

Skill/Concept

Engages mental process habitual responses using information or conceptual knowledge. Requires two or more steps.

Strategic Thinking

Requires reasoning, developing a plan or a sequence of steps, some complexity, more than one possible answer, higher-level thinking than previous two levels.

Extended Thinking

Requires investigation, complex reasoning, planning, developing, and thinking-probably over an extended period. More time is not an applicable factor if work is simply repetitive and/or does not require higher-order thinking.

COSTA'S LEVEL OF THINKING & QUESTIONING

Level 1 (literal: *"right there"*)

Remember

Show Understanding

Level 2 (analytic: *"think & search"*)

Use Understanding

Examine

Create

Level 3 (evaluative: *"I wonder or On my own?"*)

Decide

Supportive Evidence

FORMATIVE ASSESSMENT EXAMPLES

Hard copy | *Digital*

Think/Pair/Share/Write

Google Forms

3 Minute write/pause (3-fact, 2-ah-has, 1-question)

Plickers

Exit slip

Kahoot

Analogy prompt

Flipgrid

Big idea

Naiks

TRAINING & PROFESSIONAL DEVELOPMENT

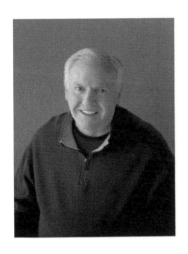

Bring Hal & *Make Waves!* to your organization, church, team, school, or district and inspire it to one of significance.

KEYNOTES, PRESENTATIONS, & PROFESSIONAL DEVELOPMENT

Hal reflects on his experience in the NFL and 30 years in leadership to deliver his unique message, to speak on living and leading. His motivational talk will leave you transformed and inspired. Join Hal on his voyage into the highs seas, leaving behind the dreary and monotonous for an amazing experience.

Hal will also train your leaders to emerge as leaders of significance in his half-day seminar. He will tailor his training to fit your specific needs.

He can also deliver his "Neurcardiologist Leader" message sharing:

- How to use emotion, movement, and many other strategies to maximize your crew's engagement
- Employ brain-friendly strategies to advance achievement and problem solving
- Use advances in neuroscience research to ignite motivation and increased performance

After hearing Hal's presentation, one principal wrote, "Everybody needs to see and hear your presentation. Thanks for touching my heart and inspiring me to continue to strive to create the environment that will foster being a wave-maker."

Another shared, "Your session inspired me."

One state educational leader at the National Title 1 conference in Long Beach told Hal, "Your session was the best one at this conference."

You can contact Hal Roberts via:

Email: pirate3314@gmail.com

Phone: (361) 446-7675

Visit his website: www.halroberts.net

Twitter: @HalLRoberts

Instagram: @hallroberts

LinkedIn: Hal Roberts

Remind: Enter number 81010 and text the message: @neurolead

REFERENCES

References

Adams, J. (2014). *Game Changers - 7 Instructional Practices That Catapult Student Achievement*. United States: Healthy Learning.

Anon, (n.d.). *Bartholomew Roberts*. [online] Available at http://www.famous-pirates.com/famous-pirates/ bartholomew-roberts/ [Accessed 29 Jun. 2015].

Anon, (n.d.). *Female Pirates Author: Krzysztof Wilczynski*. [online] Available at: http://www.piratesinfo.com/ cpi_female_pirate_women_pirate_968.asp [Accessed 16 Sep. 2015].

Blanchard, K., and Jones, L. (2002). *Teach Your Team to Fish:*

Using Ancient Wisdom for Inspired Teamwork. New York: Crown Business c2002.

Brown, B. (2018) *Dare to Lead - Brave Work, Tough Conversations, Whole Hearts.* New York: Random House

Burgess, D. (2012). *Teach Like a Pirate: Increase Student Engagement, Boost Your Creativity, and Transform Your Life as an Educator.* United Kingdom: Dave Burgess Consulting, Inc.

Cloud, H. (2013). *Boundaries for Leaders: Results, Relationships, and Being Ridiculously in Charge.* United States: HarperBusiness.

Cordingly, D. (2006). *Under the Black Flag: The Romance and the Reality of Life Among the Pirates.* United States: Random House Trade Paperbacks.

Coyle, D. (2009). *The Talent Code: Greatness Isn't Born. It's Grown. Here's How.* New York: Random House Publishing Group.

Di Giusto, S. (2014). *The Image of Leadership: How Leaders Package Themselves to Stand Out for the Right Reasons.* United States: Executive Image Consulting.

Duckworth, A. (2016). *Grit.* New York: Scribner.

Emdin, C. (2017). *For White Folks Who Teach in the Hood ... and the Rest of Y'all Too.* Random House, Inc.

Evans, J., and Jensen, E. (1998). *Teaching with the Brain in Mind*. Alexandria, VA: Association for Supervision and Curriculum Development.

Evans, T. (2012). *Kingdom man: every man's destiny, every woman's dream*. United States: Tyndale House Publishers.

Farrar, S. (1994). *Standing tall: how a man can protect his family*. United States: Multnomah Press.

FoxNews.com (2015). Trust deficit: Swing-state polls show Clinton seen as least honest candidate | Fox News. *Fox News*. [online] Available at: http://www.foxnews.com/politics/2015/10/07/trust-deficit-swing-state-polls-show-clinton-seen-as-least-honest-candidate-in/ [Accessed 7 Oct. 2015].

Gladwell, M. (2013). *Outliers*. New York: Back Bay Books.

Hammond, Z., and Jackson, Y. (n.d.). *Culturally responsive teaching and the brain*.

Kaufeldt, M., and Gregory, G. (2015). *The Motivated Brain: Improving Student Attention, Engagement, and Perseverance*. United States: Association for Supervision & Curriculum Development.

Kohler, G., Burgess, S., and Burgess, D. (2014). *P Is for Pirate: Inspirational ABCs for Educators*. Ed. United States: Dave Burgess Consulting, Inc.

Levy, B., and Leach, M. (2014). *Geronimo: Leadership Strategies of an American Warrior*. United States: Gallery Books.

Lewis, M., and Leach, M. (2011). *Swing Your Sword: Leading the Charge in Football and Life*. United States: Diversion Publishing (NY).

MacArthur, J. (2010). *Called to lead*. Nashville: Thomas Nelson.

MacNeil, K. (n.d.). *The wine bible*.

Maiers, A. (2012). *Classroom Habitudes: Teaching Learning Habits and Attitudes in 21st Century Classrooms*. United Kingdom: Solution Tree Press.

Maxwell, J. (2013). *How Successful People Lead: Taking Your Influence to the Next Level*. United States: Center Street.

MindShift (2015). *If We Know Play-Based Learning Works, Why Don't We Do It?* | *MindShift* | *KQED News*. [online] Available at: http://ww2.kqed.org/mindshift/2015/10/07/if-we-know-play-based-learning-works-why-dont-we-do-it/ [Accessed 8 Oct. 2015].

Payne, K., and Sommers, W. (2000). *Living on a Tightrope: A Survival Handbook for Principals*. Highlands, TX: Aha! Process.

Rath, T. (2007). *Strengths Finder 2.0: A New and Upgraded*

Edition of the Online Test from Gallup's Now Discover Your Strengths. 1st ed. New York, NY: Gallup Press.

Roberts, H. (2016). *Pirate on!*. United States: Tate Publishing & Enterprises.

Sousa, D. (2003). *The leadership brain*. Thousand Oaks, Calif.: Corwin Press.

Staff, C., and Sprenger, M. (2010). *The leadership brain for dummies*. United Kingdom: John Wiley & Sons.

Stanford-Blair, N., and Dickmann, M. (2008). *Mindful leadership: a brain-based framework*. 2nd ed. Thousand Oaks, CA: Corwin Press.

Twitter Direct Message, (2014). [TV program].

Whitaker, T. (2002). *What Great Principals Do Differently: Fifteen Things That Matter Most*. 1st ed. Larchmont, N.Y: Eye on Education,

Wilkinson, B., and Kopp, D. (2006). *Secrets of the vine*. Sisters, Or.: Multnomah Publishers.

Willis, J. (2009). *How your child learns best*. Naperville, Ill.: Sourcebooks.

OTHER EDUMATCH TITLES

Journey to The "Y" in You by Dene Gainey
This book started as a series of separate writing pieces that
were eventually woven together to form a fabric called The Y
in You.

The Teacher's Journey by Brian Costello
Follow the Teacher's Journey with Brian as he weaves together the stories of seven incredible educators.

Divergent EDU by Mandy Froehlich
The concept of being innovative can be made to sound so simple. But what if the development of the innovative thinking isn't the only roadblock?

Level Up Leadership by Brian Kulak
*Gaming has captivated its players for generations and
cemented itself as a fundamental part of our culture. In order
to reach the end of the game, they all need to level up.*

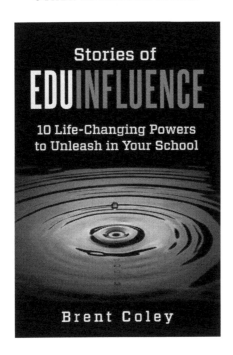

Stories of EduInfluence by Brent Coley

In Stories of EduInfluence, veteran educator Brent Coley shares stories from more than two decades in the classroom and front office, stories illustrating the life-changing power we possess.

The *Edupreneur* by Dr. Will

The Edupreneur is a 2019 documentary film that takes you on a journey into the successes and challenges of some of the most recognized names in K-12 education consulting.

In Other Words by Rachelle Dene Poth
In Other Words is a book full of inspirational and thought-provoking quotes that have pushed the author's thinking, inspired her, and given her strength when she needed it.

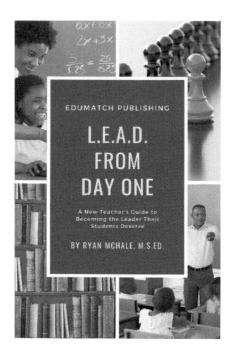

L.E.A.D. from Day One by Ryan McHale

Anyone working within the confines of a school can be a
leader. It doesn't matter if you're a baby-faced, brand new
educator fresh out of college or a seasoned veteran who's only
a couple of years away from a well-deserved siesta on a
gorgeous beach far from the nearest classroom. YOU can be a
teacher leader!

EduMatch Publishing

Made in the USA
Columbia, SC
20 December 2022

74721824R00135